I AM
HILLTOP

ANTHONY CRAIN

ISBN 978-1-63961-468-4 (paperback)
ISBN 978-1-63961-469-1 (digital)

Christian Faith Publishing, Inc.
832 Park Avenue
Meadville, PA 16335
www.christianfaithpublishing.com

Printed in the United States of America

I Am T-Town Crew
I Am a Soldier
I Am in Recovery
I Am My Brother's Keeper
I Am Blessed
I Am Hilltop

To my rib, queen, best friend, soul mate, better
half, Nubian princess, heart, protector, motivator,
inspiration—my wife, Aprile Jordan-Crain.
To my children Anthony II, Alyxandor, and Laura Crain.
To my brother, Kenneth LaRue Crain, who always believes in
me and inspires me to pursue greatness in everything I do.
To my sister, Starlene Waiss, who accepts,
respects, and loves me unconditionally.
To my fathers LaRue Crain Jr., Les Jordan, and Lionel Swift
Sr. These three Men taught me to believe in myself, never give
up on my dreams, and to work hard but enjoy my family.
To my mothers Delores Crain, Catherine Jordan,
Elenora Swift, and Mary "Ginger" Waiss. These women
influenced me to treat all women with dignity and
respect and to always honor GOD's daughters.
Trust, Loyalty, Community, and Hilltop Respect to the T-Town
Crew: Anthony Crain, TaDarwin Hardy, TaDarryl Hardy, Curtis
"Rafa" Dudley, Anthony Young, James Cain, Joseph Bellamy,
Ricky Johnson, Troy Bailey, Mike Hopkins, Ron Thomas Jr.,
Charles Jones, Phil Anderson, Theron Taylor, and Rodney Jones.

I beseech you therefore, brethren, by the mercies of GOD, *that ye present your bodies a living sacrifice, holy, acceptable unto* GOD, *[which is] your reasonable service.*

(Romans 12:1–2)

CONTENTS

ACKNOWLEDGMENTS

I have been blessed with an ability to inspire, motivate, and lead others only because I have been inspired, motivated, and led by some of the most profound, intellectual, GOD-fearing men and women throughout my life. I sincerely understand where all of my blessings have derived from, but I also know that the Lord places people in your life for a reason—that being good, bad, or indifferent. It is only appropriate for me to recognize some of the people that contributed to me, sitting down and putting pen to paper, fingertips to keypads, and allowing beautiful memories of my past to overshadow some of the misfortunes associated with my choices throughout life. My gratitude reminds me of the following Bible verse: *"In everything, give thanks: for this is the will of GOD in Christ Jesus concerning you"* (1 Thessalonians 5:18).

I would like to acknowledge my sobriety mentors, Mr. Clarence Harris of Richmond, Virginia, and Mr. Morgan Moss of the Center for Therapeutic Justice. These gentlemen taught me to never place expectations on others—you will only disappoint yourself—and always strive to make a difference not only in people's minds but also their hearts. Mr. Kevin Ryan for his unconditional love, inspiration, and support in sobriety.

I would like to thank all of my family and friends from Hilltop, Tacoma; East Side, Lakewood; Spanaway, University Place; Bremerton; Puyallup; Seattle; and across our nation.

I extend my sincerest condolences to all our Hilltop families who have lost a loved one to crime, violence, drugs, alcohol, accidents, illness, disease, or natural causes.

I salute all of my brothers and sisters in arms I served with in the United States Army, Air Force, Navy, and Marines. I would also like to acknowledge the New Equipment Training team for all of your personal and professional contributions to the readiness of our U.S. Armed Forces.

I will always honor, respect, and salute the warriors of the Quick Reaction Force I was deployed with to Iraq: Herschel Gillins, Christopher Sibley, Kenneth Pecor, Todd Bourque, Knowledge Green, Jarrod Sartini, Steven Fief, Clayton Kloehn, Chase Feener, Jasen Pfuntner, Jamell Woods, Jess Counts, Nelson Olivencia, Eric McPherson, Jared Jarorzowski, Jonathan Galicia, Brian Savage, Timothy Carter, Larry Thomas, Matthew Frank, , Thomas Hyson, Rodney Hunt, John Oxendine (RIP), Willington Rhoads (RIP).

I would like to take a moment to recognize a few warriors, first and foremost, my grandmother Jeannie M. Cooks who lost her battle with cancer. She was an amazing queen and a matriarch of our family. My aunt Mable Cooks-Dawson, aunt Estelle "Loretta" Sager and Tracie L. Davis Rest in Peace.

I am also proud of the following people who have battled and will eventually win the war against cancer because of their faith in GOD: Glenda Frazier, Linwood Lawson, Veronika Davis, Anna Cooks-Ellis, Cindy Marshall, Nic Lacy Sr., Andre Ridley, Lola Bailey, Ben Alaalatoa, Ramona Phillips, Veronica Brady, and TaDarryl Hardy.

Finally, I would like to acknowledge a handful of men and women of GOD who contributed to my awakening to the Bible, which contributed to my understanding of the following Bible verse:

> *My people are destroyed for lack of knowledge: because thou hast rejected knowledge, I will also reject thee, that thou shalt be no priest to me: seeing thou hast forgotten the law of thy GOD, I will also forget thy children.* (Hosea 4:6)

GOD bless Mrs. Sylvia Jones, Mrs. Loretta Douglas, Mrs. Mary Easter-Daniels, Mrs. Deborah Crain-Nixon, Mrs. Anna Cooks-

Ellis, Mr. Grady L. Cooks Jr., Mrs. Sondra Cooks, Mrs. Gertha Lovett, Mrs. Vernessa Ryan, Bethlehem Baptist Church, Reverend Dr. Freeman S. Rhoades, "The Muffins" (Mrs. Martha Nash, Mrs. Doty Toliver, Mrs. Marty Brown, Mrs. Debbie Marks, Mrs. Alyce Glasser, Mrs. Anne Waller, Mrs. Delmatine Ray, Mrs. Barbara Minnis, and Mrs. Althea Jones), Bishop Curtis E. Montgomery and Dr. Elinor Montgomery, Mrs. Diana Miller, Mr. Darrell Williams Sr., Mr. Roger O. Laskey, Mr. Harold Moss, Mr. Willie Hadley, Mr. Sam Daniels, Reverend Clarence Pettit, Reverend Joseph A. Boles, Reverend Ernest S. Brazill, Reverend Freddy Davis Sr., First Lady Veronika Davis, Bro' Toney Gray, Reverend Dr. Eric Jackson, Mrs. Dora Jackson, Bishop Freeze, Reverend Gregory Christopher, Bishop Michael Doss, Reverend. Dr. Anthony Young, Pastor Bryan and Pastor Kelly Briggs, and Destination Church.

I did not forget You! I just have a lot of significant people in my life. Please do not be upset by the fact that I was unable to list every single person who has impacted my life. Just so you know, I wanted to include you. Please insert your name below:

(_____).

INTRODUCTION

*Iron sharpeneth iron; so a man sharpeneth
the countenance of his friend.*

—Proverbs 27:17

My White biological mother was told that I would be adopted by a Black family in which the father was a wealthy physician, but instead I was adopted and raised by a Black family, in which my father was an electrician and my mother was an Avon representative, that resided on Hilltop in Tacoma, Washington. This family raised me to realize the importance of Christian virtues, family values, loyalty, respect, and resilience.

Collective efforts inspire unity, change, and progress, whereas selfishness breeds spite, vindictiveness, and envy. I have witnessed characteristics of greatness on many different levels throughout my life. I have always been intrigued by certain individuals willing to think outside of the box and go the extra mile to achieve unparalleled heights of the extraordinary. My fascination with success has attributed to my desires to make a difference in society. Each of us has a purpose, and this book is designed to assist you in inspiring others to identify their GOD-given talents and utilize them to increase in every aspect of their life.

My curiosities of greatness intertwined with being adopted shaped my mindset to always remember that life's current circumstances have the potential to evolve into unexpected blessings. My upbringing on Hilltop stimulated my unwavering respect for those unsung heroes willing to "stand in the gap."

The intent of the instructional theory allows the reader to create a methodical response to life's challenges and strategically develop a blueprint for personal and professional success. Many of our hidden talents require inspiration, motivation, and cultivation to materialize. Prepare to utilize your highlighter because, upon completion of each chapter, the application of the provided information is going to contribute to your new and improved transformation. Buckle up for the ride! As you read this book, you'll travel along a journey of knowledge to assist you in Conceiving, Achieving, and Believing in your ability to reach your desired destination.

HILLTOP ROOTS

And out of the ground made the LORD GOD to grow every tree that
is pleasant to the sight and good for food; the tree of life also in the
midst of the garden, and the tree of knowledge of good and evil.
—Genesis 2:9

My name is Anthony LaMont Crain. I am from 12th and Grant Street Hilltop, Tacoma, Washington. I was adopted by a loving family, Mr. LaRue W. Crain Jr. and Mrs. Athlyn Delores Crain, when I was six days old in July of 1967. I was thirteen months old when my best friend was born, my younger brother, Kenneth LaRue Crain.

My mother (Rest in Peace) a beautiful Black, full-figured woman from Shreveport, Louisiana, that was prominently affiliated with Bethlehem Baptist Church through the choir and eventually obtained the position as the pastor's secretary. Delores was a GOD-fearing woman that believed in "Family First, Family Forever." She instrumented discipline with a stern voice, belts, shoes, extension cords, and even paint-stirring paddles from Kmart. She thrived off of ensuring Kenny and I were well provided for. My mother would take any measure necessary to clothe us and ensure food was in the cabinets, refrigerator, and freezer. Considering the fact that I was a light-skinned, butter pecan little Bro' and my baby brother was a soft dark chocolate, our mother would often dress us like twins. Our mother raised us to love GOD, respect our elders, and do well in school.

LaRue (Rest in Peace), was a powerfully masculine Black man who was an athlete all throughout school—football, basketball, track, and Golden Gloves boxer served a stint in the United States Air Force and retired from the Puget Sound Naval Shipyard as an electrician.

He is my idol and epitomized a fearless Hilltop warrior. His presence was gentle but intimidating. His nickname was Killa. He instilled in my brother and me the importance of accepting responsibility for our actions and being a real man. The two biggest things my father despised were liars and thieves. He believed that through hard work, discipline, and an honest living, you could accomplish your dreams.

My childhood was complex but comprehensively nurtured by a sense of motivation to survive the inevitable challenges of the environment I was raised. As I reminisce about my childhood, there is a checkerboard of memories of the good and bad. I was adopted when I was six days old by a beautiful Black family. I was a biracial baby that was raised to love everyone without prejudice. Unfortunately, I learned at an early age that everyone was not raised with these same morals and values.

I hold a great deal of respect for the community in which I was raised. I consider it to have played an instrumental role in my courage to face challenges head on, regardless of the circumstances or preconceived uncertainties. There is an abundance of factors that have placed me into the at-risk category, but it is by the grace of GOD that I have redirected my path to navigate my way through misfortunes and missed opportunities.

Growing up in a challenging environment entailed a great deal of choices that I made as a youth that I am not proud of. In efforts to fit in, gain respect from peers, and avoid unwelcomed harassment, I engaged in some illegal activities that could have resulted in severe punishment or confinement if ever brought before a court of law.

As a teenager, I was introduced to alcohol and marijuana. Occasional use progressed into a daily use, which eventually progressed into alcohol and substance addiction which contributed to an unhealthy lifestyle of mischief and unscrupulous behaviors. I witnessed acts of violence on a regular basis within my neighborhood, at school, and let us not forget the vicious acts of violence I became habituated to viewing on television. Unfortunately, violence has the propensity to disrupt the commonalities associated with a wholesome upbringing.

I can honestly say that I did not completely embrace the importance of education until my sophomore year of high school. It was the summer of my freshmen year that I realized that if I applied myself, I could avoid a lot of the transgressions that I was responsible for. I was more aligned with establishing a reputation for being cool/tough as opposed to being academically appreciated.

I do not believe in the statement of dysfunctional families based upon the fact that every family faces various forms of challenges, difficulties, and dilemmas that fall in the category of dysfunctional behaviors. Our family was not immune to the travesties associated with the unmentionables, but I also believe that our family was able to recognize the importance of promoting family values in efforts of overcoming the inevitable challenges of my social environment. I have grown to embrace the truth in the fact that "Anything you can Conceive, you can Achieve if you Believe."

Throughout my youth, I've fantasized about being wealthy, but I learned at an early age that the only people that make a lot of money are the people that work in the Bureau of Engraving and Printing. If I wanted to be wealthy, I had to earn it. It is my belief that we grew up in the lower middle-class. The African American middle-class consisted of African Americans who have middle-class status within the American class structure. It was the societal position within the Black community that basically initiated in the early 1960s during the civil rights movement. As a young boy growing up, I was comfortable, but I was also curious as to what it would be like to live the lifestyle of those we admired on television, which happened to be nothing like what I was accustomed to on the Hilltop.

We did not have a vast amount of positive depictions of African Americans on television. It seemed as though all the good guys, superheroes, television characters of substance were White/Caucasian. Everything we associated with good in life was in comparison to a White fictional family on TV. Yes, there were several Black families portrayed on television, and these depictions of our lifestyles were presented as a source of humor. African American actors were predominately cast in the most stereotypical role imaginable. The first Black sitcom was *Amos 'n' Andy*. This provided a great opportunity for these actors, but it was not a definitive representation of our culture. It was more of a disgrace to our culture. This program utilized humor to instill the most negative depictions of African Americans conceivable.

This is how the NAACP (National Association for the Advancement of Colored People) characterized its objections to the show:

1. It tends to strengthen the conclusion among uniformed and prejudiced people that Negroes are inferior, lazy, dumb, and dishonest.
2. Every character in this show with an all-negro cast is either a clown or a crook.
3. Negro doctors are shown as quacks and thieves.
4. Negro lawyers are shown slippery cowards, ignorant of their profession, and without ethics.
5. Negro women are shown as cackling, screaming shrews in big-mouthed close-ups using street slang just short of vulgarity.
6. All Negroes are shown as dodging work of any kind.

Millions of White Americans see this *Amos 'n' Andy* picture and think the entire race is the same. (http://www.ferris.edu/HTMLS/news/jimcrow/question/oct05/index.htm)

The problem with this is that young impressionable minds, regardless of color, unintentionally and undeniably tend to buy into these portrayals as a source of reality. These preposterous stereotypes are demeaning. What is truly disturbing is the fact that some individuals fall victim to the acceptance of these appalling labels and falsehoods.

During the seventies, we were influenced and impressed with the Black sitcoms that revolutionized America's views of the African American families. *The Jeffersons, Sanford and Son, What's Happening!, That's My Mama,* and *Good Times.* We definitely must acknowledge some of the prominent movies from back then: *Shaft, Cleopatra Jones, Which Way Is Up?, Buck and the Preacher, Sounder,*

Super Fly, Foxy Brown, Willie Dynamite, Black Caesar, The Mack, Car Wash, Mahogany, Uptown Saturday Night, Cooley High, and *The Wiz* just to name a few.

As a culture, we looked at George Jefferson as someone we could relate to in that "you can take a brother out the hood, but you can't take the hood out the brother." More than any other Black actor on television, I believe the man I could most find refuge, strength, and belief in was James Evans in *Good Times*. This strong Black man was the epitome of the depiction of a Hilltop father. If ever I was required to choose an actor that reminded me of my father, there is no question as to how I would respond.

On the big screen, we were introduced to blaxploitation as pimps, pushers, hustlers, and other relative characters. Most of these characters did not represent the masses but magnetized the audience's acceptance because of their willingness to stand up to the establishment of wrongdoing. Shaft was a smooth Black omnipotent private detective that was revered as one not to be messed with who possessed the ability to appeal to the ladies and serve raw justice. Foxy Brown uplifted the women's confidence through her portrayal of a Black female superwoman willing to utilize all of her assets to defeat her adversaries. What the opposition failed to realize was that in addition to her black beauty, she was proficient in hand-to-hand combat. We, as African Americans, beheld these cinematic heroes as our response to the ill-treatment we endured over the years in Hollywood and, more importantly, in reality.

I would like to invite you into a time when the music played a major role in our cultural influences. The artists communicated our struggles, beliefs, and portrayals of circumstances in the African American communities.

"What's Going On" and "Let's Get It On" by Marvin Gaye, "Me and Mrs. Jones" by Billy Paul, "Rock With You" by Michael Jackson, "Papa Was a Rollin' Stone" by Temptations, "Superfly" by Curtis Mayfield, "Close the Door" by Teddy Pendergrass, "Always and Forever" by Heatwave, "One Nation Under a Groove" by Funkadelic, "For the Love of Money" by The O'Jays, "We Are Family" by Sister Sledge, "Shining Star by Earth Wind & Fire, "Best of My Love" by The Emotions, "The Ghetto" by Donny Hathaway, "Rapper's Delight" by The Sugarhill Gang, "Strawberry Letter 23" by Brothers Johnson, "Float On" by The Floaters, "Lean on Me" by Bill Withers, "Good Times" by Chic, "Smiling Faces Sometimes" by The Undisputed Truth, "Brick House" by Commodores, "Flash Light" by Parliament—these are only samples of the music from the seventies that shaped residents of Hilltop and American minds across the nation. The music during this era was not only relevant but positively significant. We considered it soul music, which later evolved into rhythm and blues.

We can also give Redd Foxx, Rudy Ray Moore "Dolemite," Flip Wilson, and Richard Pryor much respect for allowing us to love, understand, and laugh during a time when it was difficult to laugh.

Unfortunately, positive, productive, inspirational depictions of the African American family did not materialize until the eighties. The Huxtables exposed America and abroad to a family that represented more than what they were accustomed to seeing on television—Cliff, the father, Doctor Huxtable; Claire, the mother, a lawyer; college bound children with family values, direction, and insight to opportunities for success. Over the years, there has been improvements as to our representation as a culture and even superheroes, for example (Black Panther), but unquestionably, the stereotypes and prejudices still exist.

I grew up with several complexes—i.e., I was a skinny, light-skinned, freckled face, biracial kid who loved his family with all of the heart that pumped the red blood through his body. However, as a very young boy, I remember constantly being questioned as to why my brother and I were not of the same complexions. One day, my mother explained to me at a very young age, that I was adopted. This answered a lot of questions, but it also surrounded me with several locked doors with absolutely no keys to open them. As I grew older, I sought different locksmiths. Some doors required larger keys than others, some doors required multiple keys. To my surprise, information was provided upon request. My mother shared just enough information with me to allow my wife, Rib—soul mate, best friend and the list goes on—"Aprile" to eventually crack the safe of this mystery.

After ten years of research and detective work, Aprile was able to locate my biological mother, Mary, which led to me finding out that I also have a sister, Starlene, in addition to a niece, Elizabeth, nephews, Caleb and Nathan, an uncle, Jimmy (RIP), Aunt Stacy, Aunt Frankie (RIP), and the list goes on and on. The joy of unlocking doors that have been locked for over thirty years is unbelievable. The thought of having two loving families is amazing. Of course, I was in search of a fairy tale ending, which is why it is called a fairy tale. My biological mother eventually explained to me why she felt it was in my best interest to allow a Black family raise me. In the sixties, times were turbulent especially for interracial relationships. Regardless of why I was put up for adoption, at least I was not aborted. When I take into consideration the fact that her choice to give me up for adoption was GOD's way of giving me a little brother, Kenny, whom I love more than life itself.

My mother Delores and my mother Mary eventually were able to meet, and Mary thanked my mother for doing a wonderful job raising me. I believe that was a very difficult meeting for both ladies, but GOD created a bridge of love and respect for each of them to cross. This reunion was a blessing. It was also difficult in many different ways, trying to accommodate and accept the fact that I now have two families. The most incredible fact of this entire matter is my mother Mary, at one time, lived right next door to my dad's first cousin, his best friend "Sonny" Leonard Kelly (RIP). When I take into consideration all of the times Kenny and I went over Sonny's with my dad and watched them work on cars and drink and play cards and the very thought of my biological mother living right next door is unbelievable. I sincerely believe in my heart that GOD had a plan and purpose for my life. Who am I to question the Grand Architect Of The Universe. I am thankful to be able to say I still have two loving families that has evolved into one, and I would not trade nor change anything about my life because my mother Delores taught me, "Family First, Family Forever."

I consider myself to be a product of my environment, a product of Hilltop, Tacoma, Washington. Hilltop is a distinctive location that is recognized by many not only as their home but their roots, their foundation, their motivation and strength.

The Hilltop Neighborhood is a historically diverse neighborhood in the Tacoma, Washington Central District.

The National Register of Historic Places (US Department of the Interior) specifies the geographic area of Hilltop as located within the city of Tacoma and bounded on the east by Tacoma Avenue South, on the north by Division Street, on the west by Sprague Avenue, and on the south by the edge of the bluff, which roughly equates to South 27th Street. Hilltop derives its name from its location on a high bluff overlooking Commencement Bay and the Port of Tacoma.

Hilltop is near the historic Tacoma Public Library main branch, Bates Technical College, the Pierce County Courthouse, and the new Pierce County Correctional Facility, all of which are located on Hilltop's east side. It is adjoined by Tacoma's more affluent Stadium District.

Hilltop has been notorious for drug-related gang activity, most notably related to the infamous Hilltop Crips. The word "Hilltop" became synonymous specifically with Tacoma's gang problems and more generally with urban pathologies associated with the US's crack epidemic.

The Hilltop gained a reputation for drugs and violence with the Mother's Day riots in the 1970s. In the early 1980s, Tacoma Civic Leaders sought federal dollars by accepting a large number of Cuban Refugees. Circa 1984, an unknown Los Angeles Crip association began organizing local Hilltop youth to sell primarily powder and crack cocaine. A yearlong violent struggle ensued. Eventually, Cubans involved in the drug trade were murdered or left town. By September 23, 1989, the Hilltop Crips had become powerful, with violence and homicides at a peak, and police departments overwhelmed. The Hilltop made national news in 1989 when several US Army Rangers got into a shootout with gang members in what came to be known as the Ash Street Shootout.

Neighborhood watch efforts, increased police presence, commercial real estate development efforts along Martin Luther King Way, and rising real estate values in all areas adjoining downtown Tacoma have served to lower the amount of crime in Hilltop. However, Hilltop continues to have a high crime rate.

The neighborhood's population is approximately 12,002 and remains racially diverse. About 41% of residents are White, 30% Black or African-American, 12% Asian, 3% Native American, 1% Pacific Islander, 3% from other races, and 8% from two or more races. Hispanic or Latino of any race were 7% of the population. 32% of residents were below poverty line.

In 2007, the Tacoma City Council adopted new official boundaries for downtown Tacoma, which included a portion of the Hilltop neighborhood as far west as South L Street and changed the name of the Hilltop business district to the Upper Tacoma Business District.

In 2011, the City Council recognized that Upper Tacoma was no longer Upper Tacoma. The Hilltop Business Association (formerly the Upper Tacoma Business Association), led by President

Eric Crittendon, reclaimed the name "Hilltop," purchased new stationery, and installed Hilltop banners along Martin Luther King Jr. Way. (Hilltop Neighborhood, Tacoma, Washington from Wikipedia, the free encyclopedia)

There are several depictions, descriptions, and interpretations of the Hilltop, and I am not in a position to challenge, clarify, or communicate other resident's relationship with the Hilltop. I am willing to provide you a portrait of the lifestyle painted by many, understood by few, and appreciated by the true.

My reputation on the Hill is signified by my loyalty, friendships, and connection with other Hilltoppers that were present before the gang activity ever existed. I was cool with Hilltop Crips and Hilltop Bloods, I had family on both sides. I was most notably recognized as one of the T-Town Crew members that won "The Dog" dance contest at Skate King that drank and got high and was down to throw them hands if necessary. Life on the Hill caused us to grow up fast, and most of us earned our stripes in the streets, but most of us were looking for a new life far away from the streets.

Hilltop is not just a location, zip code, or municipality, Hilltop is a noun and a verb, Hilltop is an emotion, Hilltop is failure, Hilltop is success, Hilltop is love, Hilltop is hate, Hilltop is home. Every state, every city has a Hilltop; everybody has a choice, will you remain mentally on Hilltop, or will you go to the top of the hill?

I attended DeLong Elementary, Principal: Dr. Dolores Silas, Hunt Junior High School, and graduated from Henry Foss High School in 1985. My memories associated with DeLong are positive with the exception of some events that I believe I have harbored entirely too long. I am proud to say that I have recently released the resentment that I have stored inside of my heart for decades.

When I was in the third grade, my teacher, I will refer to her as Mrs. Scratch, would pull my hair (Afro). She would also have me sit in a refrigerator box as a form of punishment. These forms of punishment affected me significantly. I never informed my parents that I was subjected to this type of punishment out of fear that I would receive additional punishment at home. It was not until many years later that I realized that this mistreatment and inappropriate conduct was not suitable punishment for a third-grade child. Bottom line, this is one of my biggest regrets in that I did not share with my parents what was taking place at school. This fortunately did teach me to communicate with my children to never be afraid to share with me or their mother any form of punishment that they experience in school, whether it is cleaning the chalkboards, detention, or any form of physical contact.

It is imperative that our children understand the importance of communicating daily events that have occurred during school. If we develop a pattern of communicating daily activities at an early age, it will continue throughout middle school and high school. We, as parents, must utilize open-ended questions which in turn require an acceptable answer, which forces the child to use their personal knowledge or feelings.

I've learned the benefits of not just asking the monotonous question of "How was school today?" vs. "Tell me something you learned today" or "What's your personal opinion of how today's lesson will help you in the future?" We have a responsibility to our children to remain involved in every aspect of their education. Yes, the teachers are in the profession of educating our children, but parents are responsible for modeling the roles of their children. We, as parents, must accept the challenge of inspiring academic excellence in every aspect of our children's development. Education is a three-legged stool—Student, Teacher, Parents.

My parents consistently involved my brother and me in intramural athletics during our elementary school years, which evolved into involvement throughout our teenage years as well. This was very exciting and rewarding. We played basketball, baseball, and football. We played soccer from fourth to sixth grade. Our coach, "Steve Estep," would drive to the Hilltop and pick up my brother and I for practice and games in his baby blue Volkswagen Beetle with the miniature soccer ball hanging from his rearview mirror. This young White coach was in his mid-twenties and loved children almost as much as he loved soccer. His devotion to picking us up to ensure we were involved was impressive and something that I have never forgotten. Kenny was even afforded the opportunity to go to Canada and play soccer through an athletic exchange program. He was able to go stay with a Canadian family for couple of weeks, and then a young Canadian boy came to live with our family for a couple of weeks. I remember the coaches would say Kenny has a "helluva left foot." Our involvement in various sports activities contributed to our socialization skills and interaction with children from different backgrounds.

Due to my increased mischievous behavior in the fourth grade, during fifth grade, my mother sent me to live with my aunts Anna-Mae and Mable in San Diego, California. Me and my cousins, who I considered my little brother and sister—Dale Cooks and Tami Mitchell—attended Audubon Elementary. My teacher Mrs. Bailey was the first teacher to teach me Black history education that was beyond the level of the average curriculum. She was very thorough, which contributed to a new truth in my understanding of the history of the United States. She inspired us as kids to love everybody and pursue our dreams with tenacity.

During my attendance of middle school Hunt Junior High, I began to develop into a mischievous young teenager. I was easily influenced and willing to do anything to fit in. During the beginning of my seventh-grade year, I was magnetized to the older crowds, and for some reason, I was able to communicate on their level based on neighborhood experiences on Hilltop. It was not until the end of that school year that I began to surround myself with friends comparable in age. This was a notable part of my life in which I developed some relationships that have played a pivotal role in the development of my life. During this period, I also engaged in some activities that were problematic as well, I was suspended from Hunt Junior High School, a total of eight times for various acts of misconduct, kicked off the football team for possession of marijuana, got into a couple of fights, and started to realize that I may fit the description of a menace to society. I did not understand the value of education, discipline, or respect. I was more interested in proving to my friends that I was cool and down for whatever. I was sort of an "Eddie Haskell" in the presence of my friend's parents, but most of them could read right through my deceptive facade of a courteous, respectful law-abiding young man.

In all actuality, that is exactly what I was, an illusory young man. You see, ever since I was a young boy, I was just a kid trying to be cool that was down for whatever. Remember, I am from the epicenter of Hilltop, 12th and Grant. If you looked at a topographical map, our block was almost dead center of the Hilltop. Our front yard was the football field, baseball field, soccer field, dodgeball field. Our neighborhood grew up playing outside sports, riding bikes, building clubhouses, bike ramps, drinking water from the water hose, climbing neighbors' trees to eat their apples, cherries, pears, and plums, watching cartoons on Saturdays. We changed out of our school clothes and into our play clothes, and of course, we had to be in the house when the streetlights came on. These were normal everyday activities that we engaged in as youth. As we approached our teenage years, we began to experiment with drugs and alcohol, nothing too serious, just weed and beer, which later evolved into wine, liquor, and other substances.

I believe it was during the transition from my freshmen to sophomore year that I began to seriously engage in the use of alcohol and marijuana. I actually experimented before this time, but by the time I was in the tenth grade, I was seasoned, and I began to define new relationships with those who participated in these types of extracurricular activities. I formed alliances with a lot of people that were older than I was, and this proved to work in my favor in acquiring the drugs and alcohol my friends and I desired.

During the early eighties, the beer of choice was whatever we could get our hands on, but the overwhelming preference was Olde English 800 in the form of a 40 oz. drink. Throughout the '80s, the 40 oz. of Olde English 800 was single handedly responsible for more than 95 percent of the good, the bad, and the ugly memories associated with the Hilltop. I can still imagine that refreshing taste of the first sip hitting the back of my throat before I passed it to my friend on my right or left in the 40 oz. pinwheel circle as we watched to ensure no one backwashed. Absolutely nothing compared to the enjoyment of a young teenager hanging out with friends, sharing some ice-cold forties of Olde "E" and a bowl of some fresh green. There were several other malt liquors of choice (e.g., Colt 45, Schlitz malt liquor bull, Mickey's, King Cobra, St. Ides, Hurricane, Private Stock, Steel Reserve 211, and even Magnum. I hereby confirm Olde English 800 was the primary seller during the '80s. It was evident that malt liquor brands of alcohol capitalized on the lucrative benefits within the Black communities across the nation, and this definitely included the Hilltop. It also is not far-fetched to state that alcohol in addition to drugs has contributed to the consumption of a lot of Hilltop dreams, goals, and accomplishments.

Hilltop has been recognized for a lot of positive things to include the People's Center, formerly named the Malcolm X Center, McCarver Elementary, Stanley Elementary, Bryant Elementary—all of these organizations hosted recreational activities for the youth that created strong bonds throughout the community. One of the most significant in the earlier years was a place that was established in 1940. The Tacoma Boys Club on Twenty-Fifth and Yakima Street was the first and one of the most noteworthy establishments in the Hilltop community. I was privileged to be able to visit the TBC occasionally but not as often as I would've liked. Our father spent time there as a young boy. My brother and I spent time there. More importantly, a host of Tacoma Legends spent time there to include some of America's famous boxers.

"Sugar" Ray Seales, (born September 4, 1952 in Saint Croix, US Virgin Islands) was the only American boxer to win a gold medal in the 1972 Summer Olympics. As a professional, he fought middleweight champion Marvin Hagler three times. He is also the former NABF and USBA middleweight champion. Seales was born in the US Virgin Islands where his father, who boxed in the US Army, was stationed. The Seales family moved to Tacoma, Washington in 1965. He was a product of the Tacoma Boys Club amateur boxing program and was coached by Joe Clough.

Rick "Rocky" Lockridge (born January 30, 1959–February 7, 2019) (RIP) is an American former professional boxer. He is best known for handing Roger Mayweather (April 24, 1961–March 17, 2020) (RIP). His first defeat—a first-round knockout in just ninety-eight seconds, earning him the WBA super featherweight title. He later won the IBF super welterweight title. Lockridge started boxing as an amateur out of the Tacoma Boys Club being one of four world champions to originate from Tacoma.

Freddie Steele (December 18, 1912–August 22, 1984) (RIP) was a boxer and film actor born Frederick Earle Burgett in Seattle, Washington. He was recognized as middleweight champion of the world between 1936 and 1938. Steele was nicknamed "The Tacoma Assassin" and was trained by Jack Connor, Johnny Babnick, and Ray Arcel while in New York. He also appeared as an actor in a number of Hollywood films in the 1940s, including Preston Sturges's *Hail the Conquering Hero.*

Leo Randolph (born February 27, 1958 in Columbus, Mississippi) is an American former boxer, who won the Flyweight Gold medal at the 1976 Summer Olympics. Randolph had an outstanding amateur career. Randolph was a product of the Tacoma Boys Club amateur program. Randolph was trained as an amateur and professional by Joe Clough, the head trainer at the Tacoma Boys Club. In 1975, he was the National Golden Gloves Flyweight champion. He was a National AAU flyweight champion and was the 1976 Olympic Flyweight gold medalist.

Johnny "Bump City" Bumphus (August 17, 1960–January 31, 2020) (RIP) of Tacoma, Washington, was a boxer who was world light-welterweight champion. Bumphus began boxing as an amateur at the age of eight out of the Tacoma Boy's Club Boxing Club, located on 25th and Yakima Avenue, and finished his amateur career at 341–16. Bumphus qualified at 139 pounds and was a member of the 1980 US Olympic boxing team, dubbed as "Bump City." Bumphus began his professional career as a hot prospect, winning his first twenty-two fights, including the vacant WBA light-welterweight title with a decision win over Lorenzo Luis Garcia in 1984.

Emmett "Laser" Linton Jr. was born on February 21, 1971. Linton won the Junior Olympics at 100 lbs and 119 lbs in 1985 and 1986. He represented the US in the 1990 Goodwill Games in Seattle, Washington after winning the United States National Boxing Championships. Emmett won various dual meets against Korea, Italy, and Russia in which he was the only American to beat Russia. Russia seized eleven victories, and Emmett was the only American to give the US a victorious bout in Spokane, Washington. He turned pro, signing with Donald Curry as his manager and boxing phenom Bob Arum. Emmett was consistently showcased on ESPN after establishing an impressive record of 17–0. He was also featured in a top prospect article in *The Ring* magazine. While pro, he was able to capture four titles in total with two being world titles. WBU/IBA world junior middleweight title. For the WBU title, he beat "undefeated" Steve Martinez. For the IBA title, he beat Donald "Cobra" Curry who was once the undisputed welterweight champion of the world in the eighties. Emmett continues to stay involved in the profession by conducting boxing classes and training sessions to increase young athletes' strength and conditioning through the disciplines associated with boxing. He is the brother of fellow boxers Maurice and Robert Linton, and he continues to strive to make a difference in the Tacoma community.

Mylon "Kid USA" Watkins—Watkins was the 147-pound Golden Gloves champ as well as 1983 US junior and junior world gold medalist. He had an outstanding amateur career and was the winner of the 1984 National Golden Gloves welterweight championship and the 1985 and 1986 National Golden Gloves light middleweight champion. Watkins turned pro in 1987 and won his first two pro bouts but soon after, retired. Mylon was truly recognized throughout the entire Hilltop community as a boxing legend with limitless potential. He is loved by all, and his contributions to the boxing community is a positive reflection on Hilltop and the city of Tacoma, Washington. (Wikipedia, the free encyclopedia)

In 1981, the Al Davies Boys & Girls Club was built and located at 1620 South Seventeenth Street, directly adjacent to Stanley Elementary School, four blocks straight down the street from my house. Al Davies served as a facelift for the Tacoma Boys Club. Al Davies was and still is instrumental in the development of youth in the Hilltop community. In every community, children strive to build relationships through good, wholesome recreation in their neighborhood. Al Davies served as a nucleus for the youth of Hilltop to congregate for youth activities, tournaments, sports, community events and occasional weekend dances. Al Davies was basically an after-school care program for a lot of children in the area.

My first job ever was babysitting my younger cousin Nicholas for my aunt Debbie Crain. My first official job was my paper route, delivering newspapers for the *Tacoma News Tribune*, Route 107-05 and Route 107-07. This job taught me the importance of work ethics, responsibility, and financial discipline. Customers relied upon me to deliver the latest and greatest source of local, international, business, political, weather, and sports information. I accepted the responsibility of picking up a bundle of newspapers and inserts "advertisements" and delivering them to assigned residents in a timely manner daily. I was then responsible for collecting payments from the customers in which my assertiveness and persistence was tested. My communication skills allowed me to convince my customers that I was respectful but adamant about receiving payment on the appointed day of collection. Customers did not concern themselves with the fact it was raining, hailing, or snowing. They expected their newspaper to be delivered, which contributed to my self-discipline, doing the right thing regardless of the circumstances. While a lot of my friends were out having fun in the neighborhood, I was on my route fulfilling my obligation. My paper routes consisted of several housing residents surrounding my home but also the senior citizens' homes on 12th and M Street. This allowed me to meet some truly great people and develop some lasting relationships. Eventually, I passed this job on to my younger brother.

I was constantly seeking involvement in community-related opportunities and ultimately got a job at the Al Davies Boys & Girls Club. I initially served on the youth council, and I was actively involved in volunteering for various activities, which led to me being offered a position as a youth programs coordinator. Don't laugh; I earned a meager $0.50 an hour, $18 every two weeks. I was extremely disciplined with my budget of this hard-earned check. I would spend $5 on a half gram of weed, $3 on two 40 oz. bottles of Olde E, and I would save $10. This budget not only became a ritual, but lo and behold, it also taught me how to save my money in order to acquire items of interest. Believe it or not, this budgeting opportunity also taught me to be responsible, be accountable, and strive to be better through financial discipline.

Two very prominent people associated with the Al Davies Boys & Girls Club during the early eighties was Mr. Elmer Dixon and Mr. Roger O. Laskey. Mr. Dixon was the director and Mr. Laskey was the assistant director. Elmer Dixon played a major role in the advancement of young African Americans through motivation and inspiration. His overall accomplishments and contributions to the civil rights movement were immeasurable. Mr. Laskey played a central role in the Hilltop community as a member of the NAACP and as a member of the Prince Hall Free and Accepted Mason fraternal organization.

Both of these gentlemen promoted the importance of recreational activities and companionships; but more importantly, they both inspired the youth to remain actively committed to their educational goals, in addition to some other adults at Al Davies, Tom L. Mustin, Leo Randolph, Emmett Linton Sr., Rodney Clark, Eugene Mobley, Jimmy Irving, Elliot Wooten, Lionel Swift, Robert Swift, Irvin Hooper, Kenneth McDuffie, Byron Jordan, David Stewart, Nicole Stewart- Smith, Tonya Wilson, Jessica Fletcher, Anthony Gallion, Dowell Williams, Delma Williams, Joy Netter, Jacki Weston, and the list goes on. For this very reason, I will continue to uplift and promote the importance of supporting our Boys & Girls Clubs across the United States of America but definitely the Al Davies Boys & Girls Club.

We must prioritize educational goals and pursue them persistently. Education can be utilized as a bridge to prosperous transformations. My appreciation for education has grown over the years. When I was a sophomore at Henry Foss High School, I failed to acknowledge the importance of education. My goals consisted of establishing a reputation, hustling, partying, and illegal activities.

It was not until my mother expressed her genuine disappointment in my overall performance or lack thereof. I agreed to attend a summer class offered by Bates Vocational Institute. It was a carpentry course at the former Woodrow Wilson High School now honorably renamed Dr. Dolores Silas High School. This was the beginning of my personal interest in achieving my goal of graduating from high school. It was not until my junior year of high school that I realized that if I kept my mouth shut, displayed respect for the teaching staff, and went to class I could graduate. What is truly disturbing is the fact that it took me so long to realize that if I applied myself, I was capable of achieving my goals. This attributed to me developing a sense of respect for academic achievements and the opportunities associated with scholarly efforts.

So basically my tenth-grade summer, I enrolled in a carpentry class to earn additional credits, which led to me enrolling in a welding course at Lincoln High School in the eleventh grade. I would attend Foss in the morning for my core classes and Lincoln in the afternoon for vocational trade classes. I also selected elective courses to serve as a teacher's assistant in some educational lab classes to earn additional credits. The only reason why I was allowed to serve in this capacity was because I turned over a new leaf and attempted to demonstrate a new level of respect for the teaching staff, but it was difficult to see a fellow student walk by the classroom see me, and they would assume that I was actually in that particular class as opposed to serving as a student assistant. This perception challenged my pride, but my determination to achieve my goal of graduating allowed me to dismiss their perceptions and focus on the celebration. My senior year, I enrolled once again in the carpentry class at Wilson, which allowed me to meet the love of my life, my wife, Aprile. My mistakes in the tenth grade contributed to my decisions to pursue creative measures to achieve my goals, it also allowed me to attend different high schools in Tacoma, which in all actuality increased my education and vocational knowledge, skills, and abilities.

I personally witnessed classmates, peers, and relatives work toward their academic goals in efforts of graduating and pursuing future educational endeavors. I realized during my junior year of high school that my parents were not in a financial position to finance any college aspirations, but in all fairness, I never really expressed a sincere interest in a college education, nor was I pushed, persuaded, encouraged, or influenced to pursue a college degree by my parents or academic advisors. I honestly believe that my parents and I were basically content with me graduating and receiving my diploma. It was not until later in life that I realized the benefits, necessity, and importance of higher education. Life lessons and aspirations influenced Aprile and I to eventually pursue and attain our associate's and bachelor's degrees.

I attribute my ability to face difficulties, struggles, and challenges that I encountered while growing up on the Hill to my undeniable persistence, drive, and dedication to working hard to achieve my personal and professional goals. My Hilltop hunger played a vital role in me pursuing employment opportunities, which sustained my choices and decisions as young man seeking the American dream. As previously mentioned, I began dating Aprile in High school, and we have been together ever since. We both graduated in 1985. She graduated with honors. We gave birth to our first son, Anthony II, in 1986, which basically stifled her college aspirations. This also inspired me to take responsibility for my actions in order to provide for my loved ones.

I worked two jobs. I was a subcontractor for the Tacoma Urban League that landscaped in the city of Tacoma and surrounding areas, during the day, for ten to twelve hours, and I performed janitorial work in the evenings. This enabled Aprile and I to get our first one-bedroom apartment in Lakewood, Washington. We eventually moved into a two-bedroom apartment in Tacoma, and soon after, we were pregnant with our second son, Alyxandor LaRue, and the following year, Aprile joined my hand in marriage on December 26, 1987 at Bethlehem Baptist Church, officiated by Reverend Dr. Freeman S. Rhoades. The following year, November 1988, I enlisted in the United States Army.

My departure for the Armed Forces was a pivotal point in my life due to the ever-present increase of gang related activity on the Hill. My departure contributes to my longevity. I grew up with family and friends on both sides of the flag of Bloods and Crips. If I would have remained in T-Town during the height of attraction to the gang life, my days may have been numbered. I earned my respect on the Hill by sharing knowledge with young brothers in efforts of building character and upholding the code. Unfortunately, the introduction and infiltration of crack cocaine instigated the demolition of family structure, brotherly love, and social integrity. Boys grew into men overnight, especially after the killing of Bernard Houston, a close family friend of my wife, Aprile, as a child. Aprile's mother, Catherine Jordan, and Bernard's mother would visit each other's house often to socialize and play cards. When this incident occurred, the gloves came off, and Hilltop Crips were spellbound with the thought of hood justice. The only problem was, the victims did not always claim a red or blue flag; victims regrettably included innocent bystanders, the parents, grandparents, families, and friends who suffered the loss of their loved ones. This upsurge of violence on the Hilltop was responsible for the initial stages of destruction of a community within T-Town, also known as the City of Destiny.

When I returned home after attending Basic Training, Airborne School, and Advanced Individual Training, the Hilltop had evolved into a highly respected Hilltop Crips empire, substantiating my decision to pursue greatness, beginning with redefining my purpose.

My love for my community has always been genuine and unconditional, but my love for my family has inspired me to seek self-improvement through personal and professional growth, which contributed to me reading the book *Think and Grow Rich: A Black Choice* by Dennis Kimbro and Napoleon Hill. This book was beyond enlightening. One of the most inspirational quotes that I read in this particular book, which has become my personal motto, is "Anything I can Conceive, I can Achieve if I Believe." Let me explain…

Hilltop Thoughts:

- The Lord is thy consultant.
- Familiarize yourself with positive change.
- Our current physical locations can be substituted with desired mental locations. We may physically be in a location of negative, but we possess the ability to mentally travel to a positive destination.
- We can change like the wind freely or remain stuck like a rock wedged in by surrounding pressures.
- We desire to be familiar. We want others to know who we are by what we have accomplished, achieved, and possess. We should familiarize ourselves with the unfamiliar desires of faith, hope, charity, and wisdom.
- We must be willing to live, learn, and love. We must be willing to grow spiritually through aggressive change.
- Scientific studies have absolutely nothing to do with me. I am the Lord's experiment.
- Explorers embarked upon new heights without knowledge of their destinations. As I explore my faith, I have realized I am destined.
- We tend to build fortresses around our hearts to defend against hurt, sadness, disappointment, and pain. If we surround our fortresses with Jesus, we will be protected by love, happiness, blessings, and faith.
- Stampeding horses magnify the sound of power and direction. We have the ability to allow the clueless to learn from our stampeding efforts to make a difference.

BE ALL YOU CAN BE

*Blessed be the Lord, my strength, which teacheth
my hands to war and my fingers to fight.*

—Psalms 144:1

When I was a teenager growing up on Hilltop, we did not like the soldiers from Fort Lewis now referred to as Joint Base Lewis-McChord. We didn't call them soldiers, we called them GIs. We didn't like them coming to our neighborhood driving around in their new fancy cars, playing loud music, talking to the girls. In all actuality, we were "Haters." We were jealous of them coming to our neighborhood, dating the local girls. We would actually wait for them to come to one of the corner stores at either 15th or 19th and K Street—now it is MLK Street—but we would wait for them to walk outside the store, and we would compete to see who could knock the GI out with one punch. Sometimes we found out that all GIs were not punks, and they were ready to throw them hands. That did not stop us from terrorizing any foreigners on the Hill. This was not something I am proud of. Eventually as time passed, we began to accept the fact that some of these guys were actually good people, just trying to live their life away from home. Who would have ever thought at that time that I would eventually enlist in the United States Army and become what I despised—a GI.

I was twenty-one years old when Aprile and I were pregnant with our second Son, Alyxandor. Our firstborn, Anthony II, required growth hormone shots that cost in excess of $1,100 a month, and I was not in a financial position to sustain this financial responsibility by working at Auto Lube ten-minute oil change. I needed a job with medical benefits, and the military appeared to be my best option. At this particular time in my life, Aprile and I were attending Bethlehem Baptist Church regularly. Life was moving in a positive direction for both of us.

On my birthday, July 12,1988, my father asked me to drive him to Bremerton, Washington, to pick up his new Z/28 Camaro. Once he came outside with the keys to his new vehicle, he handed me the keys to his 1978 Camaro, and he told me, "Happy birthday." I drove back to T-Town happy as could be. I went to pick up Aprile and the boys because I was scheduled to meet with the US Army recruiter to discuss my options for enlistment. It was on this special day that I was informed by the recruiter that I could not join the Army due to the fact that I was charged with a felony as minor for a physical altercation I was involved in as a teenager. I was heartbroken. May I remind you that my oldest son, Deuce required growth hormone shots, and I was making less than $10 an hour. We drove back to our apartment. After I stopped crying and I pulled myself together, I called a recruiter for the U.S. Marines. I inquired about enlisting. I informed the recruiter that I had a felony.

He said, "No problem." He asked me if I was married.

I said, "Yes."

He said, "No problem."

He asked me if I had any children.

I said, "Yes."

He said, "No problem."

He asked, "How many children do you have?"

I said, "Two."

He said, "Problem. You cannot enlist in the United States Marine Corps as a private with two children."

As I hung up the phone and I sat in my bedroom alone, the tears flowed without sound. I felt as though I would not be able to provide for my family financially and provide my Deuce the medical prescriptions that he required. I eventually presented all of this information to my mother Delores, and she, of course, told me to pray on it and leave it in the Lord's hands. Well approximately one week later, my mother called me and asked me to come to her house so we could talk. Well she informed me that she shared my story with one of the deacons at the church, and he explained to her that since I was charged with a felony as a minor, I should be able to pursue having my records sealed once my restitution was paid in full. I had always assumed that my parents had already paid my restitution, but this was only an assumption and definitely not true. I eventually did my research pertaining to the amount owed to the local juvenile institution, Remann Hall. Aprile and I paid the restitution, and my juvenile record was permanently sealed. The following day, I went to meet with a different Army recruiter at a new location, and he explained to me my options. I really did not care what the Army wanted me to do, I just wanted medical benefits for my family and an opportunity to be a good provider. I had to pass the ASVAB test (Armed Services Vocational Aptitude Battery exam). I also had to take a physical. I knew that I had not smoked weed for about a year, so I was confident I would pass the physical in which of course I did. However, while I was at the MEPS (Military Entrance Processing Station) in Seattle, Washington, awaiting the approval of my waivers due to my criminal history I required about eight to ten waivers to enlist, sitting in a waiting area reading a magazine, I looked up, and all of a sudden I just so happened to see one of the Army recruiters from the first recruiting station walk into the room, and he looked me straight in the eyes as if to say, "I know you have a felony, why are you here?" I began to sweat and pray at the same time, all the way up until I raised my hand and said, "I, Anthony LaMont Crain, do solemnly swear that I will support and defend the Constitution of the United States against all enemies, foreign and domestic, that I will bear true faith and allegiance to the same, and that I will obey the orders of the President of the United States and the orders of the officers appointed over me, according to regulations and the Uniform Code of Military Justice. So help me GOD."

Before I go any further, allow me to inform you, the United States Armed Forces is not for everyone. I respect every American citizen's freedom of choice. This is why I encourage anyone considering the military to pray, research, and speak with veterans before you enlist. Many young recruits join for various reasons, patriotism, college, financial opportunities, medical benefits, citizenship, the reasons may differ nonetheless. Our military has been a voluntary force since the '70s. Regardless of the reason young men and women choose to enlist, the fact remains: everybody is not built to serve in the armed forces. I encourage any and everybody considering joining the military to do their research and definitely talk to family and friends. Yes, of course you will need to eventually meet with a recruiter who will discuss with you all of your options, but this does not stop you from doing your research prior to meeting with the recruiters.

First and foremost, consider if you would like to serve as an enlisted or as an officer. Do not assume that because you did well in school, you are prepared to take the ASVAB. It is imperative that you study and take preparation examinations with your high school career counselor or at the local library. This is very important. Your career options will be based upon how well you score on this exam. Your willingness to prepare accordingly can open doors that will increase your opportunities. Ask yourself, are you mentally and physically up for the challenge? Research what occupational specialties appeal to you, and do your research on every one of them. Do not just rely upon a five-minute video to determine a choice that will affect the rest of your life. Believe me, if you take this advice, you'll thank me later. Now those of you who opt for college, vocational-technical institutes, Job Corps, entrepreneurship, or other lucrative endeavors, I wish you all the best. Just like the military, pray, research, and talk to your family and friends.

I attended basic training at Fort Leonard Wood, Missouri. My Drill Sergeants taught me discipline, loyalty, and the overall importance of values. Throughout my military career, I learned the advantages of a structured life as compared to a misguided lifestyle. My career assignments and leadership positions include Yuma Proving Ground, Arizona; Airborne Test Force, Test Jumper, Fort Lee, Virginia; 262nd QM BN, Instructor/Writer and Drill Sergeant, Fort Lewis, Washington; 2nd Ranger Battalion, Platoon Sergeant, Pusan, Korea; 4th QM Detachment, First Sergeant, Fort Bragg, North Carolina; XVIII Airborne Corps, Platoon Sergeant/

First Sergeant, Okinawa, Japan; Eighty-Seventh QM Detachment, Detachment First Sergeant; 1st Battalion 1st Special Forces Group (Airborne) Detachment Sergeant. My military career has afforded me the opportunity to travel across the world and experience various cultures, philosophies, and principles.

When I initially joined the U.S. Army, the motto was "Be All You Can Be." This particular quote was self-explanatory and easily understood. This slogan inspired me to push harder, lean forward, dig deeper, and never quit. The United States military is the world's largest melting pot of citizens from every imaginable region in the world. I felt proud to be placed in a position to work collectively with individuals from who knows where to accomplish mutual goals. The military's ability to form bonds through cooperative efforts to meet shared duties and responsibilities established a sense of trust and dependency on others. My ability to embrace others and develop a clearer understanding of differences contributed to my overall respect for others regardless of their race, religion, ethnicity, sexual preference, or origin. The physical and mental demonstration of consideration for others is a valued trait and is uppermost in my beliefs. My personal insecurities have contributed to my progressive development of appreciation for variances over the years in addition to my commitment to respect the unfamiliar.

The ability to identify with others' strengths and weaknesses has enabled me to recognize personal and professional areas of potential growth. More importantly has taught me that "Teamwork makes the Dream Work." The reward of accomplishments is attributed to purpose, direction, and motivation. I believe the military has played an instrumental role in my desire to aid and assist others in their journey to identify and compromise physical, mental, and spiritual barriers. Regardless of where we hail from and the conditions surrounding our upbringing, personal determination to succeed is immune to the threatening circumstances related to social injustice, marginalization, subjugation, or socioeconomic status.

Throughout my career, I have been blessed with meeting thousands of peers, subordinates, and superiors from various "Hilltops" across our nation in addition to other countries, such as Africa,

Mexico, Puerto Rico, Trinidad, Dominican Republic, Jamaica, Thailand, Philippines, etc. During our discussions, our motives were similar in nature in that each of us raised our right hand to defend the constitution of the United States against enemies, both foreign and domestic, in efforts of providing a better life for our families. Unfortunately, we also shared a vast number of other commonalities, which included the perils of addiction, crabs in the bucket mentality, infestation of crimes in our neighborhoods, lack of local community opportunities. etc. These shared sorrows inspired us to pursue new adventures with trials and tribulations that involved separation from our families, physical, and mental challenges and risks that could result in the ultimate sacrifice. Through professional instruction, training, and confidence in our abilities, we were able to develop into leaders of soldiers that were proud to defend this country with honor.

My clear and present comprehension of the importance of education, mentorship, and goal-related benchmarks is the driving force behind the intent of this project. I, as have many others who have looked beyond the four corners of our existence on the Hilltop, have been afforded an opportunity to breathe new life into a heart that was fueled by the bondage of our neighborhood and bounties of loyalty to a location of isolation and desperation. For many years, I believed that the Hilltop was the span of the earth. Once I ventured out to explore new and exciting cities, states, and countries, I was introduced to a broader spectrum of opportunities, confidence, and interest. Yes, the military provided me housing, a guaranteed paycheck, health care, free education, paid vacation, in addition to an abundance of other benefits. The Hilltop remained ever present in my heart. I am not just referring to my family and friends but the omnipresence of Hilltop as a whole. Each of the benefits listed above were instrumental in sustaining my lifestyle and livelihood, but the benefits associated with my experiences and inspirations from Hilltop are immeasurable. My struggles and strife prepared me to "Be All I Can Be" in pursuit of my stripes. The U.S. Army's motto eventually changed in 2001 to a controversial slogan of "Army of One." But it was laid to rest in 2006 quite simply because it subconsciously contradicted the message of "Teamwork."

In 2006, the new motto was introduced and received with open arms, "Army Strong"—once again, self-explanatory and easily understood. The Hilltop is comparable to the military in that it exemplifies strength. The Hilltop has endured formidable challenges and valiant attempts to dismantle its historic urban atmosphere. We have to embody these same characteristics and remain steadfast and resilient when faced with challenges. Our display of discipline and determination will circumvent what appears to be insurmountable. Ultimately, we have to utilize strategic planning and innovative measures to rise above our current circumstances without jeopardizing our morals, values, or ethics. Each of us have witnessed greatness through the means of television, movies, internet, and even within our communities. I believe that we should take every available measure to emulate those that have epitomized perseverance when confronted with the unimaginable but imagined victory before defeat.

Throughout my military career, I have been blessed with opportunities to be recognized by distinguished attire, headgear, or badges. I enlisted to serve in the Military Occupational Specialty of an Airborne Parachute Rigger, formerly known as 43 Echo, which we referred to as 43 Everything but currently known as 92 Romeo. In order to serve in this particular MOS, you were required to attend Airborne School after Basic Training. Upon graduating from airborne school, I was presented with airborne jump wings and a burgundy beret. So as a private in the United States Army, I had achieved what many leaders had never achieved. I was "Airborne." I do not know what meant more to me, the beret on my head or the silver jump wings upon my chest. Both of these items of apparel demonstrated that I was among the best and above the rest.

I was then required to attend Parachute Rigger School. The Parachute Rigger also wears distinctive headgear. It is a red baseball cap with Rigger Wings and the individuals rank on it. So dependent upon the duty uniform, I would be required to wear either my Beret or Red Hat. While assigned to my first duty station as a Test Jumper, I was selected to serve on the Post Color/Honor Guard in which we were required to perform burial ceremonies, flag ceremonies, parades, and additional Military Honors. Serving in this capacity authorized me to wear an Honor Guard patch with my Airborne patch on the left sleeve of my uniform in addition to an aiguillette, also known as a braided cord, on my opposite sleeve.

When I transitioned permanent change of station (PCS'd) to my next assignment as an Instructor/Writer, I was awarded the title of Distinguished Instructor in which I was authorized to wear a silver badge that identified me as such. I later attended the Drill Instructors Academy. Upon graduation, I was awarded a Drill Sergeant badge and a Drill Sergeant hat. When I deployed to Iraq, I was assigned to the Quick Reaction Force, and the QRF was authorized to wear a shoulder brassard identifying us as the Battalion QRF.

As previously stated, I have been afforded the opportunity throughout my military career to separate myself as an elite soldier based upon my distinguished attire, headgear, or badges awarded over the years. I have to admit that I was motivated by the thought of exceeding the standards, striving to demonstrate to my peers, subordinates, and superiors that I was capable of exemplary performance, and my uniform was a walking resume of my knowledge, skills, and capabilities.

I still believe that it is important to exemplify your strengths through your physical presence. This can be achieved by understanding the importance of dressing for success. Civilians do not wear their resumes on their daily attire, so it is your apparel that represents you as a person. Dependent upon the situation, circumstances, or event, dressing for success has various interpretations. Taking the appropriate measures to improve your professional appearance has immeasurable benefits. Besides feeling good about yourself, favorable opinions derive from positive perspectives associated with the message you send to others by your well-groomed appearance. It is, without question, our physical appearance that plays a significant role in how others view us, both personally and professionally. The ability to grasp the importance of the image that you display personally and professionally puts us at an advantage over those who underestimate this necessity. There are several clichés pertaining to appearance—"dress for success," "if you look good, you feel good," and, my favorite, "you never get a second chance to make a first impression."

My confidence as a leader is a direct reflection of the incredible noncommissioned officers and officers that exemplify the essence of a soldier. My appreciation for their mentorship, commitment, and technical and tactical proficiency is immeasurable.

My very first squad leader, while assigned to the Airborne Test Force at Yuma Proving Ground, Arizona, was SSG Linwood Lawson. He molded me as a soldier and groomed me to become a noncommissioned officer. He taught me if you take care of soldiers, soldiers will take care of you. He was not only a professional mentor, but he has also been one of my best friends since the day I met him.

I enjoyed serving as an instructor of soldiers, NCOs, warrant officers and officers while training the Army, Navy, Air Force, and Marines while assigned to Fort Lee, Virginia. This provided me the opportunity to experience the professionalism that exists in other branches of the Armed Forces.

I can honestly say that my tenure as an instructor was fulfilling, but there was no greater feeling compared to serving as a United States Army drill sergeant. This opportunity allowed me to mold, mentor, and train soldiers to become the future leaders of our military.

I still have soldiers contact me or come up to me and say, "You were my instructor or you were my drill sergeant." Some are senior NCOs, some are warrant officers, and some have even become commissioned officers. I cannot explain the feeling you get when you realize the impact you had on so many soldier's lives.

I have had the distinct pleasure of working with several professional NCOs and officers in my career. I would be remised if I failed to acknowledge some that have left an impact on my life and also inspired me to uphold the noncommissioned officer creed throughout my career.

COL Alexander Davis (RIP), SPC Eric T. Burri (RIP), SFC Brandon K. Sneed (RIP), CW5 Cortez Frazier, CW4 Kelvin Thompson, SFC Robert Anderson, SFC Tracy Long, 1SG Perry L. Thompson, 1SG Herschel Gillins, MSG John Davis, MSG Wayne O'Connor, MSG John Jewett, CSM John Sanders, CW5 Eric Hooker, CW5 Roy Melebeck, CW4 James Hall, SGM Angelo Lindsey, SGM Clem King, CSM Danny Richards, PR1 Reggie Whitehead, SGT

Bryant Wilson, SGT Jerry Jensen, MSG Bonalyn Harris, 1SG Terry Holbert, MSG Robert Bethea, 1SG Marshall Ford, MSG William Marshall, 1SG Timothy Grinstead, MSG Tracey Madison-Grinstead, CW3 Sabrina Bentley-Thompson, CPT Shandale Hall, MSG Donald Moore, MSG Marvin Dunn, SFC Eric Wareham, MSG Jeff Grievous, 1SG Mel Carter, SFC Rono Carter, SFC Timothy Smith, 1SG Donnie James, SFC Kevin Patterson, 1SG Steve Fief, SFC Kenneth Pecor, SFC Paul Black, MSG Dannie Herron, CW2 David Bird, COL Bryce Pringle, COL Herman Johnson, CSM Anthony Boles, COL Stephen Cherry, CSM Jefferey Crawford, LTC MN Thompson-Jackson, COL Pharisse Berry, LTC Moody-Love, CSM Larry Donaldson, SGM Robert Johns, LTC Winchester Stiens, CW5 Anthony Haiduk, 1SG Christopher Sibley, CSM Frederick Baldonado, SFC Vincent Tracy, MSG Todd Borque, Chief Petty Officer Tony Futrell, SFC Michael Franklin, SFC Tony Collado, SFC Bruce Powell, 1SG Robert Bruce, SFC Sammie Patrick, CSM Mary Brown, CW4 Petrice McKey-Reese, CW4 Lazaro Street, CW4 Patrick Roper, CW4 Kevin Sims, CW4 Ordia Brown, CW2 Alex Vaquero, CW4 Brian Perinon, SFC Patrick Sornson, SFC Trey Norris, SFC Clay Wilkinson, SFC Luis Feliciano, SFC Aaron Engelman, SFC Damon Brant, SFC Michael White, SSG Lonnie Ford, SFC Alexander Pillot, MSG Jerry Smith, SSG David Porter, SSG Rodney Johnson, SFC Michael Spencer, SFC Todd Hutley, SFC Bobbie Salazar, SFC Juan Delacruz, SFC Joseph Plewniak, SFC Richard Hamm, 1SG Rob Weston, SFC Sean Hensey, SFC Eric Morris, SFC Donald Walker, SFC Mary Carter, SFC Jesus Mike Linares, SGM Earl Harold, LTC Major Johnson, 1SG Darron Britton, 1SG David Countryman, 1SG Bernard Hughes, LTC Herb Champion SFC Cooley Ingram, SSG Lesron Baker, Chief Petty Officer Shawn D. Mitchell, 1SG Larry Norwood, SFC Charles Saulter, SFC Danny Fleming, 1SG Cathy Wall, SFC Edward Crowder, 1SG Reuben Green, MSG Jacenta Sutton, MSG Deardeary Sutton, SFC Darryl Lovett, SSG Donald Martin, 1SG Terry Boddie, SFC Theaduis Prioleau, MSgt Ted Seats, SMSgt Shawn Gilmore, CMSgt Michael Brown, SGT Anthony Young.

The names I have addressed have played a vital role in the success of the defense of our nation. It is because of leaders like this that our families can sleep at night, knowing their freedom is protected.

The United States Military has provided me with several tools to face life's challenges. Without question and for all the right reasons, I will always support and uphold the significance of "Be all you can be." I will constantly challenge myself as well as my family and friends to strive for greatness. My personal and professional accomplishments are not achieved in efforts of shining but more importantly in efforts of inspiring and influencing others to believe in their own personal and professional capabilities. I have been privileged to witness greatness throughout my life, and this has inspired me to take the necessary measures to "Be all I can be," to GOD be the glory, because "Anything I can Conceive, I can Achieve if I Believe."

Hilltop Thoughts:

- Personal victory is based on our personal convictions.
- An eight-legged spider has eight opportunities to move in the right direction. We have two, so we have a fifty-fifty chance of taking the right path.
- Smiles are contagious. You have an obligation to contaminate everyone you encounter.
- Positive energy is priceless, but some of us would rather be bankrupt because we spend extravagantly on negative energy.
- Equality is symbolized by two equal lines: negative by one single line, positive by two bisecting lines. Now tell me two is not better than one.
- As I look into the mirror in front of me, it allows me to see my reflection in the mirror behind me so as to remind me that as I look forward, my past is still visible, but it will always remain behind me.
- Take the appropriate measures to accumulate the necessary tools to design the trustworthy net in preparation for that unexpected fall. No one can prepare your net for your fall better than you.
- The language, gestures, and anger utilized during road-rage can easily be substituted with forgiveness and a smile.
- The willingness to begin each day with a positive position will strategically baffle the opposition.
- Hurtful words have penetrated more hearts than bullets. Similar to a drive-by shooting, innocent bystanders become victims. Surgery cannot heal wounds caused by vocal shrapnel.

LIFE SKILLS AND PRINCIPLES

Give instruction to a wise man, and he will be yet wiser:
teach a just man, and he will increase in learning.
—Proverbs 9:9

We have a responsibility to protect our youth and young adults by any means necessary. The best method of providing protection is to afford them with the essential life skills and principles throughout life that will support and enable their self-preservation in the event of our inevitable absence. From infant to adulthood, we must continue to strive to equip our children with the necessary tools to prepare them for life's challenges. Based upon your culture, the environment in which an individual is raised in and the resources available will have a tremendous impact on the formulation of their comprehensive life skills in addition to their overall order of precedence.

Providing the appropriate life skills will position our youth with preemptive measures to face adversities with confidence. There are many skills that are taught to us by family and friends, but certain skills are self-taught through our natural born survival instincts, such as fight, flight, or freeze. When we are faced with imminent danger, our neurotransmitters and hormones kick in, distributing signals to our adrenal glands, increasing our adrenaline, causing us to respond subconsciously with one of these three protective mechanisms. Dependent upon the circumstances and our surroundings, we will mentally and physically respond according to the threat at hand. Our survival instincts play a vital role in our overall existence within society. Our life skills prepare us to respond accordingly in hopes of achieving positive consequences. Whether we are proactive or reactive, our choices and decisions will position our paths.

The foundation of our paths is paved with good direction, which is why we instill in our children the value of honesty, sharing, listening, self-discipline, respect for others, self-control, communication, etc. All of these skills, in conjunction with others, provide our children with the fundamentals that are designed to correlate with one's physical, mental, and social survival.

But it is imperative that your foundation of principles is built upon a solid ground in the same manner as any structure. A weak foundation will not be able to sustain the weight or burdens of a heavy load, inclement weather, earthquakes, stress, and increased temperatures. When we embrace the principles of a spiritual relationship with GOD, our foundation of faith will sustain us throughout life's trials and tribulations.

Build on the Rock

> But why do you call Me "Lord, Lord" and not do the things which I say? Whoever comes to Me and hears My sayings and does them, I will show you whom he is like: He is like a man building a house who dug deep and laid the foundation on the rock. And when the flood arose, the stream beat vehemently against that house and could not shake it, for it was founded on the rock. But he who heard and did nothing is like a man who built a house on the earth without a foundation against which the stream beat vehemently; and immediately it fell. And the ruin of that house was great. (Luke 6:46–49)

As we mature, we continue to expand and enhance our life skills through our morals and principles to include integrity, which contributes to the definition of our core values. When we live a life of integrity, our respect for others and self-respect become paramount, and the benefits are immeasurable. Integrity symbolizes our commitment to spiritual growth. It also earns the trust of others, and this is not easily accomplished. Integrity is a valued trait that each of us should strive to never negotiate. Let's discuss some additional skills that may be of assistance throughout life.

Creative thinking involves the art of challenging the imagination and allows us to envision various scenarios, perspectives, and alternative solutions to deliver new and improved results. This particular skill enables us to improve upon our problem-solving techniques and make creditable decisions. Everyone is not motivated enough to think outside of the box. Many of us are systematically programmed to follow the patterns of proven methods without venturing off into unknown variables. Our creativity defines our greatness through uni-illustrated shadows of new thoughts dancing around in a brain that is capable of a multitude of visions, ideas, and victories. Every traveled path was once discovered by the quest of an individual willing to experience new endeavors who placed faith over their uncertainties. When we utilize our creative thinking skills to brainstorm and formulate plans, this is how our thoughts materialize into inventions, creations, and new developments. We should not only embrace our creativity but promote the rewards associated with creative thinking.

Communication is an integral element of our life skills, and it would be to our dismay to ever underestimate the importance of being able to communicate effectively on a wide range of scales. Our overall ability to convey and collect information in a manner that is appropriate, whether it is verbal or nonverbal, plays a vital role on the outcome of personal and professional situations. Utilizing complete sentences and being able to articulate in a manner that exudes confidence and competence will open doors and also nullify stereotypes. Our understanding of the benefits related to dismantling communication barriers is vital to strengthening our social networks.

Communication is the passageway to new and improved relationships. Many of us in society have unfortunately allowed our cell phones, laptops, and social media sites to replace verbal communication. Text, tweets, emails, and Facebook posts will never replace the true essence of face-to-face personal interaction. Modern technology is unquestionably convenient, but the propensity to complicate things based upon misinterpretations can be detrimental to the intent of the conversation. Text, emails, and tweets can be informative or destructive dependent upon the interpretation of the conversation, whereas taking the time to dial a phone number or meeting with the individual directly removes all barriers and allows us to communicate effectively.

There is no substitute for looking into someone's eyes, analyzing their body language, being attentive of their vocal tone to evaluating the seriousness, sarcasm, or human emotion of the topic of discussion. Nonetheless, in order for us to improve communication on every level, once again, it begins with the foundation. We have to instill in our children the responsibility of communication. The norms have been exploited over the years. We have children texting parents and vice versa while both child and parent are in the same household in lieu of communicating face-to-face. The benefits of this new convenience have long term effects on our children's social involvement within the family, church, school, and workforce. As parents, we should consider implementing parameters on the use of these technological devices to ensure they are utilized responsibly when appropriate and in moderation. Communication is essential, and we have the ability as responsible citizens to improve it and take the necessary measures to preserve it.

Resilience defines our overall ability to respond to challenges, setbacks, and obstacles in a personal or professional setting with a strategy or proposal that reflects positive outcomes. Throughout life, we will be faced with enormous difficulties and challenges, and it is imperative that we utilize the appropriate coping mechanisms to deal with these unfavorable moments in a constructive manner and adjust accordingly.

We should be able to turn our barriers into bridges, challenges into can-dos, setbacks into setups, and obstacles into opportunities. Our inner drive and assertiveness provide us the mental stamina to keep our head up and lean in the direction of triumph. The reality of the fact is we are not born with resilience. This is a learned character trait based upon our ability to adapt to adversities. This is a promising skill that will benefit each of us throughout our journeys due to the likeliness of our encounters with hardships and misfortunes. Resilience is the definition of our character in reference to our psychological strength, our ability to sustain our faith, and maintain a "never quit" attitude. It is a testament of our resilience and fortitude.

Self-discipline demonstrates our maturity in conjunction with self-control when we recognize the benefits of making sound decisions through discipline to personally restrain our actions and comments during stressful situations. This is a representation of our personal growth, and it also contributes to our personal qualities. Whenever we witness an individual lose their cool when dealing with others, we tend to look down upon that person as someone that is out of control. However, when we are privileged to witness a person conduct themselves in a cool and collective manner during stressful circumstances, it tends to elevate our overall respect for that person whether we know them personally or they are a complete stranger. We have a strong tendency to admire an individual who displays self-control in hostile situations or circumstances.

Parenting is an inevitable life skill that many of us must undertake with only nine months to prepare. Unfortunately, a high percentage of teenage pregnancies occur that are not planned and require two parents to step up and raise their children as responsible adults. Regardless if you are a teenager, young adult, or middle-aged, it is imperative that we take every measure to raise our children to be obedient, respectful, responsible, and in accordance with GOD's will.

First and foremost, it is imperative that we recognize the fact that children are a blessing and not everyone has been afforded the opportunity to raise a child. With this blessing comes responsibility, and we should take every available measure to ensure that we are providing our children the best opportunity to succeed in life. Children utilize their five senses to adapt to life, and what we display as parents is vital to what that child will perceive to be right and wrong patterns of behavior. We must strive to demonstrate the benefits of a positive mindset versus negative actions and behaviors. Happy parents will inspire happy thoughts, actions, and behaviors in their children.

Family bonding through togetherness will enhance relationships, praying together, eating dinner together, watching movies together, reading a book or studying the Bible together, completing projects together, playing games together, all have something in common— together—and that is the recipe for a healthy relationship. Our ability to create healthy relationships at home will motivate our children to develop trusting, respectful, meaningful relationships outside of the home, which will contribute to productive relationship building, all of which brings us back to self-discipline. When our children witness this trait in us. They will understand the importance of the benefits of exercising good moral conduct in the presence of others and also in the privacy of our home. Our ability to promote the immeasurable advantages associated with optimism will definitely have a positive impact on our children. Optimism positions our children for success through a multitude of platforms to include a positive mindset, increases productivity, reduces stress, dream with confidence, use failure as motivation, promotes spiritual development, peace of mind, and self-awareness.

We, as parents, must provide our children with the blueprint map to achieve whatever their desired goals are in life. In order to do this, we must first instill in them the importance of defining their ability and willingness to grow through learning new skills. We must ensure they value the fact that "knowledge is power," and they must assume the life form of a sponge and learn as much as they can from anyone and anything willing to teach them (i.e., person, book, computer, google, and even mistakes can be exceptionally informative as long as we learn from them). Learning is an everlasting endeavor that each of us should embrace as a gift that keeps on giving.

Situational awareness is the ability to demonstrate vigilance by sustaining cognizance of the current conditions and circumstances of our immediate and pertinent surroundings. The tools required to maintain awareness involve attentiveness to the details within your environment. Our personal observations will allow us to analyze situations and formulate a conscientious assessment as to how we will respond wisely. It burdens me to make this point, but the relevance is more beneficial than the backlash I may receive. We cannot trust everyone within our circle, including family and friends. I am sure that each of us have been disappointed at least once by a family member or friend, this is not uncommon. As long as we utilize this as a teaching moment or lesson learned, we can turn the negative into a positive. Whether it was due to their actions or lack thereof, disloyalty, a lie, a loan, betrayal, infidelity, or whatever the offense may be, our situational awareness in conjunction with intuition will enable us to avoid these types of transgressions. For us who have already been victims of wrongdoings, well hopefully our new sense of insight will elevate our alertness in our dealings with family, friends, acquaintances, and most importantly strangers. Vigilance is a gift that prevents heartache, headaches, and relationship related regrets.

The list of life skills and principles can go on and on, but the length of the list does not equate to the gist of the list. Our ability to instill the importance of life skills and principles in our children, youth, and young adults can change the dynamics of society. To honor, respect, and love our fellow brothers and sisters in society will change the world, and all these virtues begin in the home. Let's make a difference by upholding our responsibility to protect our youth by promoting life principles, because "Anything I can Conceive, I can Achieve if I Believe."

Hilltop Thoughts:

- We are meticulously orchestrated instruments, designed to deliver the Lord's symphonic gospel. The family consist of strings, woodwind, percussion, harps, brass and voices. Though we are created uniquely, we each play a vital role in the composition of harmony.
- Doors enable us to lock others out or gain admittance. It is imperative that we utilize caution in whom we issue our keys to. When in question, rely upon our Father, the master locksmith.
- Athletes who have achieved championship(s) understand the importance of mental and physical preparation. In order for us to achieve our goals, we must put our life/game face on.
- A path will guide us, stairs will take us to the next level, ladders will take us to the top, but faith will take us to victory.
- There is no expiration date on inspiration.
- If you have plans to appear at the pearly gates, it is highly recommended that you make proper reservations.
- Captivate your audience as you make your entrance into a room, facility, vehicle, or vessel. Immediately place a smile on your face. The eyes of others will observe your happiness with admiration.
- Plan accordingly. We have to prepare for our landing before we can prepare to take off.
- Happiness cut in half is like a broken rainbow, there is still happiness on the other side.
- Prioritize your baggage in accordance with your personal goals. Check the wants, and carry the needs.

FAITH

*Trust in the Lord with all thine heart; and lean
not unto thine own understanding.*

—Proverbs 3:5

Our faith is the pillar of our existence. Our understanding of the immeasurable opportunities and blessings is attributed to our faith in GOD. In addition to my faith in the Grand Architect of The Universe, I strive to embrace the importance of having faith in myself. According to dictionary.com, faith is a noun, which means (1) confidence or trust in a person or thing: faith in another's ability; (2) belief that is not based on proof: He had faith that the hypothesis would be substantiated by fact; (3) belief in GOD or in the doctrines or teachings of religion: the firm faith of the Pilgrims.

"I can do all things through Christ who strengthens me" (Philippians 4:13). It is essential that I realize that faith without action is only an idea. I have an obligation to move in the direction of the identified purpose, goal, objective, desire, or blessing. Faith is a powerful tool of success that is illustrated and demonstrated by accomplishments in the physical, psychological, and spiritual sense. Our willingness to develop beliefs in our personal and professional abilities is vital to the expansion of our capacities. The principles associated with faith allow us to clinch onto something greater than our common understanding of the circumstances we face that are beyond our control.

In life, it is inevitable that we will encounter struggles and adversities. Through our faith in GOD, family, and friends, we have the ability to pull through any situation or difficulty. Our willingness to venture into a new outlook on life with positive perspectives increases our understanding of the benefits of faith. Each of us is vulnerable to the challenges of society, and it is during our weakest moments that we rely upon a greater calling than ourselves. Faith is a phenomenal instrument that relieves the burdens of stress, anger, fear, and uncertainty. My faith is greater than my fears. My comprehension of faith allows me to identify resolutions with favorable conclusions.

Fear incites false feelings of despair and discouragement, which contributes to the development of insecurities. Our ability to increase our mental stamina will enhance our confidence through concentrated efforts of courage and calculated probabilities of faith.

Every step we take in life is based upon faith that the surface beneath our feet or the opportunity in front of us is present and stable enough to sustain the weight of our next step forward. If someone asked you to be the first person to cross a bridge that was recently built, some of us would be apprehensive. Those that are familiar with the process of building a bridge understand the procedures, details, safety measures involved and have full confidence in the stability of the bridge. When we approach a bridge for the first time, we really do not know what is on the other side or what is supporting this enormous awe-inspiring apparatus that was created by a balance of considerations. What we do know is that it is designed to provide us safe passage to cross a valley, a body of water, or simply get from our current place in life to a new place in life. Bridges have proven to be brilliant solutions that enable us to cross existing obstacles.

The bridge of faith is similar. We don't always know if our faith is strong enough to get us to the other side of uncertainty. Through experience, difficulties, and painstaking moments in my life, it is my privilege to inform you that the bridge of faith was constructed by the most qualified architect of the universe. His tools are tested, directed, and respected. Everyone who has ever crossed a bridge of faith plays a vital role in building new bridges of faith of greater heights, scales, and magnitudes of greatness. Yes, when you are faced with challenges—"windy days"—the bridge will sway from side to side, causing nervousness and doubt. Rest assured the bridge of faith works by compressive forces in some places and flexible forces in others. The chances of the bridge of faith collapsing is implausible.

Our actions speak louder than words, and our faith stands stronger than our fears. Whenever we come to the realization of the rewards associated with faith, we stand a little taller, we walk a little smoother, we smile a little harder, and we live a lot longer. Unusual circumstances or unforeseen misfortunes are known as uninvited challenges. Our compressive forces and flexibility will allow our faith to supersede anything that misdirects or interferes with our purpose, direction, or happiness. I am Forever Awake In The Hope because "Anything I can Conceive, I can Achieve if I Believe."

Hilltop Thoughts:

- We must utilize the only prescribed anecdote for personal guilt. GOD's prescription for our choices, regrets, and indiscretions is confession.

- Experience today as if the doctor told you yesterday you will not live to see tomorrow.

- As the years pass, we have been introduced to new and exciting technology. It's our turn to reinvent ourselves—out with the old and in with the new.

- Dependent upon the substance utilized to inflate a balloon, it will rise to the unknown or remain grounded. Be conscious of what you inhale.

- The abilities required to adapt to change entail desire, willingness, and flexibility. Warm your thoughts so that you are flexible enough to stretch your imagination.

- I create melodic remedies with my thoughts; stay in tune. I allow my thoughts to dance to the rhythm; stay on beat. I'm preparing for a live concert; get your tickets.

- I Can if I Will.

- Technical specialists earn their titles through education, experience, and discipline. Without discipline, you are unworthy of a title.

- Education enables us to realize the motivation, dedication, and rejuvenation it requires to become an inspiration.

- The distance between me and my dream is only a goal away.

EDUCATION

The fear of the Lord is the beginning of knowledge:
but fools despise wisdom and instruction.
—Proverbs 1:7

Education is our passport to the future, for tomorrow
belongs to the people who prepare for it today.
—Malcolm X

Education is the most powerful weapon, which
you can use to change the world.
—Nelson Mandela

We must remember that intelligence is not enough. Intelligence
plus character—that is the goal of true education. The
complete education gives one not only power of concentration
but worthy objectives upon which to concentrate.
—Martin Luther King Jr.

Education is that whole system of human training within and
without the schoolhouse walls, which molds and develops men.
—W. E. B. Du Bois

Education is the key to unlocking the world, a passport to freedom.
—Oprah Winfrey

Once you learn to read, you will be forever free.
—Frederick Douglass

The absence of understanding the essence of opportunities through education is a miscalculation of the perils of bondage. Our youth have been victimized by the illicit presence of a disturbing tolerance for their ignorance, disrespect, and ungraciousness. Our children face critical challenges that many parents have never experienced, and the pressures of growing up in today's society is more troubling than we are willing to admit. Many parents believe that there is nothing our children can do that we have not already done. I can assure you that this is far from the truth. Social media, Facebook, Twitter, Snapchat, and Instagram, just to name a few, did not exist prior to the year 2000. Our children have embarked upon a new wave of information, communication, and social identification.

When our children are born, they are angels with boundless potential. We have a duty and responsibility to nurture our seeds with love, morals, and values to blossom into greatness, but our society has allowed political turmoil, social media, crime, violence, drugs, and alcohol to infiltrate the minds of our adolescents. A tremendous number of our children from underprivileged communities to include Hilltop and across the nation underestimate the significance, value, and power of education.

I have come to realize that we, as parents, have to instill the importance of capitalizing on the benefits of proven education.

Unfortunately, more than sixty years after Brown vs. Board of Education, our education systems nationwide are separate and unequal. For this very reason, we, as parents, must be intimately involved in the academic policies, performance, and progress of our children. We can no longer fall victim to the belief that it is acceptable to simply wake our children up for school, feed them, and rush them off to the bus stop. We cannot expect our educators to provide them with all of the essential tools of self-discipline, perseverance, and goal-oriented behaviors. This is our responsibility. This is our onus. We must give our children the best tools available. Education is a three-legged stool—teacher, student, parent. The absence of commitment from any one of these three can be detrimental to the overall success of the student.

When we take into consideration all of the foreign exchange students who come to America through varying circumstances to achieve their dreams through educational prophecies leading to success, it is imperative that we take the appropriate measures to instill in our youth as early as conceivably possible the importance of educational opportunities.

Our children require purpose and direction. We have the ability to inspire them through wise counsel and consistent demonstrations of involvement in their path to success. We must assist our youth in their efforts to surpass our expectations through discipline and determination.

The acronym EDUCATION means

Elevation

Determination

Uplift

Confidence

Aspirations

Transformation

Inspiration

Optimism

Never Quit

Booker T. Washington placed a great deal of emphasis on African American's survival and safety. He understood the importance of self-esteem, self-actualization, and belonging, but these concerns were secondary.

Once the basic needs were met, then they could focus on economic independence, home and land ownership, and starting a business. The humanistic efforts of adult educators, like Booker T., placed the personal needs of the learners first. Learning for personal change was a secondary but essential characteristic of adult education. Washington recognized the disadvantages associated with African Americans and advocated for our people to embrace the benefits of industrial opportunities through related education. He believed this form of instruction would greatly increase their opportunities to position themselves strategically in the social, political, and economic structure of America.

W. E. B. DuBois believed in self-help for African Americans and understood the social dynamics that race played in America for Blacks. DuBois's answer to the problems that confronted Black America was the power of education to transform the race, in contrast to Booker T.'s humanistic philosophy. DuBois was concerned with the activism that African Americans needed in order to gain social and political freedoms. In other words, he did not want to wait to meet survival needs first but was more militant about the need to demand one's rights. He understood the interplay of race, economics, and education and the conflicting feelings many Blacks had of being an American and being Black. DuBois's self-help philosophy is therefore more aggressive than Booker T.'s. As with the work of Booker T., DuBois's book, *The Souls of Black Folks* (1903), can be regarded as one of the early books on self-help education in America because it promotes survival skills acquired through education.

We must study the ways in which African American adults pursue learning that facilitates personal growth and self-help and can lead to self-actualization. Given the strong need for self-help education in the lives of African Americans, adult education cannot continue to ignore this area of adult development and learning in America. Adult educators can contribute to and enhance the area of self-help education by exploring essential questions and assisting adults in critically selecting and analyzing self-help literature to maximize their learning experiences using these books as a resource.

References:

Denton, V. L. Booker T. *Washington and the Adult Education Movement.* Gainesville: University Press of Florida, 1993.

DuBois, W. E. B. *The Souls of Black Folk.* New York: American Library, 1969. (Originally published 1903.) (http://www.ericdigests.org/2001-3/african.htm)

Education plays a pivotal role in the development of our youth and their ability to mature into positive and productive citizens within their community and in society as a whole. Our ability to emphasize the benefits of scholastic accomplishments will cultivate a disciplined mentality and genuine appreciation for the opportunity to attend prestigious educational institutions. Less fortunate disadvantaged children in foreign countries embrace educational opportunities and are willing to go to great lengths to be selected to attend school locally or abroad. We have to develop this same amount of passion and drive in our youth through motivation, inspiration, and positive associations. Educational opportunities reside in the sheer determination to develop skills, knowledge, and capabilities through intensive learning. When a child demonstrates the discipline to immerse themselves into academics, the benefits are immeasurable to include scholarships, corporate-driven internships, and international occupational assignments.

Malcom X stated that "education is our passport to the future." What is a passport? A passport identifies you and allows you to travel internationally. A passport will enable you to journey from one place to another, from familiar to distant unfamiliar destinations. Education is a passage to the unknown.

Nelson Mandela implores us to arm ourselves with the most formidable defense available—education. Every willing and able-minded individual should strive to possess this weapon of mass production through systematic instruction.

Intelligence is developed in many forms and by different means, but Martin Luther King Jr. reminds us that "intelligence is not enough." Martin's wisdom enlightens us to the importance of accompanying intelligence with character. This is accomplished through education. Proven intellect establishes a sense of credibility that is clearly respected when adorned with nobility.

Throughout life, we should constantly endeavor to achieve greatness through personal and professional growth. Striving to meet benchmarks, achieve goals, and compromise obstacles are the educational tools of human training that contributes to the beliefs of W. E. B. DuBois of how education transforms us into accomplished men and women.

Everything of the world that is associated with value is usually protected either by code, secret, or lock and key, and in many cases, some or all of these protective measures are applicable to education. Knowledge is power, education is valuable, and this substantiates Oprah's philosophy that education is the key to unlocking the world. We have been born as locksmith apprentices, and it is our responsibility to become a journeyman locksmith with several keys to unlock a vast number of passageways to new heights and the freedoms of learning.

I would like for you to look at the two *oo*'s in the word "look." Now look again and view them as eyes looking back at you with admiration and respect. Look at what you are doing right now. Look, you are reading, you are increasing your intellect, you are pursuing personal and professional growth. We are all familiar with the slogan "reading is fundamental," but the discipline to read has somehow, over the years, become more and more uneventful. Whereas when we take into consideration the fact that, at one time in our history, it was a crime for a Black person to attempt to read or attempt to educate themselves, the possession of literature could result in severe punishment and in some cases death. History reminds us of the sacrifices our ancestors made to educate themselves by any means available to them. Their quest for knowledge was undeniable because they were fully aware of the benefits associated with education. According to Frederick Douglass, who realized that reading was a psychological vehicle to freedom, "Success requires solutions. The ability to mold our children into greatness is the core of academic answers. The "three-legged stool" supports parental enthusiasm for scholastic achievements, which will inspire the necessary heartfelt appreciation for learning. Family members and friends also play a pivotal role in acknowledging the significance of growth through continued sources of learning.

Our willpower to succeed must be in alignment with developing a strong sense of admiration for success through education. Our family, friends, and loved ones are responsible for nurturing our youth with information that will provide them the means to survive in society. "Give a man a fish, and you feed him for a day. Teach a man to fish, and you feed him for a lifetime" (Chinese Proverb).

African American heroes have emphatically expressed the importance of education throughout history, and it is our responsibility to uphold and respect their plights to pave a path to physical and psychological freedoms by means of education. Foreigners embrace hope for an opportunity to come to America and achieve their personal and professional dreams through education. We must update our passport, load our weapons, and concentrate on academic objectives throughout human training with the keys to success by continuing to learn through reading and embracing the empowerment of education because "Anything I can Conceive, I can Achieve if I Believe."

Hilltop Thoughts:

- We have to feed, nurture, and respect our passion in order for it to grow into fruition.
- Stop thinking, wondering, and doubting if it will; start believing, knowing, and claiming it will.
- Only a woman can give birth to a child, but anyone can give birth to a dream. It may take nine weeks, nine months, or nine years, but once it arrives, it will be a bundle of joy.
- Nominate yourself to accomplish, achieve, and acquire your needs.
- A positive description of yourself is depicted by your lifetime subscription to positivity.
- The man who commonly utilizes all five senses usually understands those who lack common sense.
- Thoughts + Emotions + Choices + Behaviors = Future
- Our ability to meet future challenges depends upon our willingness to challenge our current abilities.
- Even the Man of Steel has a weakness. Our strength is our ability to identify ours.
- Positive Impression: I'm Pressing On.

GOALS

*I press toward the mark for the prize of the
high calling of GOD in Christ Jesus.*

—Philippians 3:14

How do we keep hope alive?—by "**G**iving **O**ur **A**spirations **L**ife **S**upport." We must breathe life into our success. The strength of goal-setting is reliant upon an individual's commitment to personal and professional objectives. The absence of goals defines a lack of effort, exertion, and earnestness, which results in a recipe of missed opportunities. We must strive for greatness through strategic processes and procedures of utilizing achievable benchmarks as motivation to seize the moment.

Goals are recognized as conceived resolutions to achieve intended outcomes or results. It is imperative that we identify and implement short-term, midterm, and long-term goals in efforts of positioning ourselves for success. Our ability to orchestrate a continual path of growth must be accredited to synchronizing the short-term goals in a sequential formation that will transform into the long-term goals. We must compartmentalize our everyday tasks and incorporate the appropriate measures to thrive though purpose and persistence. Our purpose substantiates our reasoning for completing objectives in correlation with our intentions. Purpose enables us to commit ourselves to a task or objective that is motivated by an uncompromising sense of self-fulfillment. Persistence pertaining to goals is nonnegotiable. It is imperative that we remain steadfast and determined to cross the finish line. Our ability to definitively align our goals will greatly enhance our potential to endure the struggles and embrace the rewards associated with success.

Identifying goals must be calculated through intentional measures that will contribute to the materialization of the desired results. The most common process involves the acronym SMART:

*S*pecific: Goals must be precise, explicit, and definitive.

*M*easurable: Goals must me perceptible, quantitative, and calculable.

*A*chievable: Goals must be possible, viable, and attainable.

*R*ealistic: Goals must be rational, relevant, unpretentious, and down-to-earth.

*T*imeline: Goals must be time-bound, have a reasonable time-table.

Write your goals down and protect your goals with all your heart. Your goals are personal and should only be shared with family members and friends that will support your dreams. Do not advertise your goals with pessimists, also known as haters. Goals are for winners, champions, leaders, and trailblazers. Everyone does not possess the discipline, motivation, or willpower to create and pursue their goals with purpose. Your goals are the seeds to your future. The more you nurture them, the greater chances for them to eventually flourish. Your goals are your future based upon your ability to prophesy your success and take the appropriate measures to achieve them.

Inscribe your goals in your heart, soul, and mind. Infuse your goals into everything you believe in. Embrace the success that accompanies the accomplishments of victory. It is imperious that you believe in your ability to attain your goals. Place a realistic value on each goal, and be willing to pay the expense necessary to own it. Goals are expensive. If you are not willing to pay the cost of disappointment, rejection, or failure, you cannot afford success. Rest assured that you can finance your dreams through discipline, determination, and a desire to win at all costs. Formulate your goals in the same manner as a general in the military strategizes his war plan. This is recognized as backward planning.

The well renowned Stephen Covey also introduces the strategic concept of backward planning in *The 7 Habits of Highly Effective People: Habit 2: Beginning with the End in Mind.*

> To begin with the end in mind means to start with a clear understanding of your destination. It means to know where you're going so that you better understand where you are now so that the steps you take are always in the right direction. (franklincovey.com)

This is basically a strategized plan of events that will systematically strengthen our chances for success. When we are able to realize the significance of our *goals*, we will be more inclined to pursue them with tenacity. Strive to embrace the importance of your goals, and this will fuel your persistence to meet the end state. Whether you take the time to create a well-orchestrated vision board or simply taping a picture of the house of your dreams on your bathroom mirror or kitchen refrigerator/ It really does not matter as long as you are willing to take the appropriate measures to ensure your goals are SMART because "Anything I can Conceive, I can Achieve, if I Believe."

Hilltop Thoughts:

- My Vision usually consists of things I can't physically see.
- The objective is to surprise the enemy before the enemy surprises you.
- Hard work strengthens our root cause.
- My resilience will not allow my past the privilege of navigating my future.
- You will receive unexpected blessings when you perform unexpected acts of kindness
- During your victory lap, remember to acknowledge your supporters and your haters.
- Guidance is best utilized when we are willing to dance in step with the guide.
- Framed artwork was once just a canvas without boundaries.
- The ability to connect requires a willingness to reach beyond touch.
- The three-point line has increased in distance over the years to increase the challenge. Our challenges should increase over the years to increase our existence.

BUDGETING

But seek ye first the kingdom of GOD and his righteousness;
and all these things shall be added unto you.
—Matthew 6:33

The familiarity with the word *budget* tends to weaken the importance of its intended value within our lives. Many of us understand the definition of the word *budget*, but many people fail to recognize the monetary benefits of financial discipline. You do not have to be a financial expert to implement some budgeting savviness into your lifestyle. Financial security is something that we all strive for daily. The sooner we introduce ourselves to a productive budgeting plan, the sooner we will reap the benefits of our applied efforts.

A personal budget can be described as identifying a fairly accurate estimation of income in addition to personal expenses during a specific period of time. Once this information is gathered, it is strongly recommended that you utilize something in the form of a notepad, spreadsheet, computer program, or budgeting website to maintain and sustain a disciplined budget. The more stringent your budget principles, the quicker you will attain your financial goals and dreams. Our ability to effectively manage our revenue and expenses is critical to the development of disciplined life skills. Implementing the appropriate time management skills and practicing budgetary measures will eventually pave our paths to financial freedom.

Budgets are instrumental in the developing stages of disciplined behavior. It's definitely not easy, but nothing worth fighting for ever is. That is why so many people fail because they are intimidated by the challenge or too lazy to invest the time. Your willingness to devote the time to establishing a budget will be rewarded with greater financial opportunities.

It is better to create a simplified budget as opposed to no budget at all. As you begin to grow with your finances, you can research and commit to a more comprehensive budgeting system. We can begin by utilizing a basic spreadsheet by annotating our monthly expenses, regardless of what it is. If you have a weekly, monthly, or annual financial obligation, include it on this spreadsheet. To make things as simple as possible, you can round up to the nearest dollar. Once you have established all of your expenses on your spreadsheet, now you can proportion your income accordingly. Best case scenario, your income will exceed your expenses, but if this is not the case as previously stated, we will adjust according to prioritization in relation to essentials and nonessentials. Tithe 10% Non-negotiable, off the top Tithe. Do not even think about it just Tithe! Essentials: 50% of income will be proportioned to housing, utilities, groceries, hygiene, transportation, insurance, and childcare; 10%–20% to retirement savings; 10%, incidentals; 10%, leisure activities. All of these figures are adjustable according to your individual circumstances, but we must govern our finances with confidence in accordance with the benefits of discipline.

One of the most effective methods of remitting payment to debtors is electronically or online payments. These allow you to track your payments and alleviate you of unnecessary burdens to include gas, stamps, and envelopes. Automatic payments correspond with your disciplined commitment to your financial obligations. Some people prefer to write out checks. Any form of record keeping measures is commendable and should be practiced with conviction.

Cash versus credit cards is a personal preference dependent upon your level of discipline and financial requirements. Maintaining a specified amount of cash for incidentals or leisure activities is appropriate when the determined amount is not excessively exceeded or not in alignment with your short- and long-term goals. Credit card discipline is critical and must be adhered to at all costs. We must ensure that we undeniably maintain control over our credit card nonessential expenses.

As previously mentioned, time management will play an important role in our budget planning process. We are encouraged to commit a minimum of fifteen to thirty minutes a week to our financial goals by updating our budget spreadsheet or computer program to sustain accuracy and up-to-date records. This minimal amount of time each week can prevent fifteen to thirty months or even years of unnecessary debt. Preferably, the allotted time will be documented and consistent on a regular basis to establish a structured program that will enhance your budgeting experience. Your willingness to verify income, expenses, paid expenses, as well as performing inquiries pertaining to financial discrepancies are essential tasks that will support a strong foundation of financial discipline.

The information provided is designed to elevate our overall understanding of the available tools necessary to effectively manage our money regardless if it is $50, $500, or $50,000. The majority of us realize the significance of utilizing the services of a financial advisor if we are ever placed in a position, whereas we are responsible for a large sum of money. We must remember that if we are unable to effectively manage smaller denominations of money responsibly, it is highly unlikely that we will practice financial discipline with larger denominations of money. Now is the time to develop our financial savviness, which will inherently expand with our net worth through financial discipline and blessings because "Anything I can Conceive, I can Achieve if I Believe."

Hilltop Thoughts:

- Attack each hurdle one at a time. Stay in your lane. The quicker you get over it, the quicker you can focus on the next hurdle.
- Productive thoughts evoke productive results.
- Failure to observe could result in failure.
- We have a choice to accept or decline defeat.
- The fragrance of fear evaporates with a touch of faith.
- Uncleanliness can be remedied with a spiritual shower.
- An open mind will turn an obstacle into an opportunity versus a closed mind will turn an opportunity into an obstacle.
- A standing eight count allows us to recover, collect our thoughts, and to protect ourselves to prevent getting knocked out. Don't be afraid to stop and start counting.
- Focus less on being a victim of circumstances, and focus more on the victories attributed to second chances.
- Alive is a life that minimizes the thought of surviving and maximizes the thought of thriving.

DISCIPLINE

*Love not sleep, lest thou come to poverty; open thine
eyes, and thou shalt be satisfied with bread.*

—Proverbs 20:13

Discipline equates to "doing the right thing when no one is looking."
Throughout life, we will be presented with immeasurable opportunities, choices, and decisions. Our ability to make the right choice in
the absence of direction, guidance, and control measures will demonstrate the presence of our defined principles with relationship to the
various levels of discipline. We are taught during our infant years the
difference between right and wrong, what to do and what not to do,
what is acceptable and what is not acceptable. Our comprehension of
conforming to the established norms of right and wrong encourages
us to comprehend and comply with guidelines, rules, and provisions.
Our willingness to disregard the importance of compliance is also
representative of our individual mindset.

Disciplined behavior is a commendable trait that enhances
our personal and professional character. The presence of a disciplined individual invokes a sense of respect and confidence in their
abilities and perspectives. We are defined by our thoughts, actions,
and behaviors. When we can articulate our reasoning and demonstrate our intentions, motives, and decisions through choreographed
choices, we substantiate our focus. Discipline deters us from life's
distractions to include enticements and pleasures and allows us to
sustain our focus on goal-oriented objectives.

It is imperative that we implement the necessary tools to establish guided principles that will aid and assist in goal-driven objectives. Some individuals require external incentives, motivation, and encouragement, and then there are those who personally create internal motivation through personal incentives to establish, pursue, and achieve their personal and professional objectives. Our individual ability to demonstrate self-control is representative of our maturity and respect for others in addition to self-respect. Discipline can manifest positive results through inner strength when battling life's challenges to include procrastination, addiction, and chaotic circumstances.

Self-discipline enables us to avoid the temptations associated with failure or substandard performance. A mental state of mediocracy can lure us into traps of complacent patterns of behavior. It is essential that we remain steadfast and determined to fend off the opposition by arming ourselves with confidence, conviction, and the ability to make command decisions. Discipline does not allow us to put things off until tomorrow when we can do them today. The absence of discipline breeds incompetence and inferiority complexes, which contributes to the lack of self-esteem, doubt, and uncertainty. If you happen to see a person drop their wallet, phone, or $20 bill on the ground and you secure the item from the ground or capture the individual's attention and inform them that they dropped their belongings, this is a commendable display of integrity and discipline.

Our attitude is the continuity between responsible conduct and self-discipline. We must be accountable for our actions and embrace the importance of responsibility. Responsibility is defined by our ability to respond accordingly to challenges and dilemmas. Our attitude must align with our individual purpose through self-control. It must also coincide with strong organizational skills that parallel the ability to focus.

A structured lifestyle alleviates the manifestation of unnecessary stress. Our ability to implement the necessary changes in our lifestyle that will prevent undue tension or aggravation is a step in the right direction. We must uphold and support the tenants of goodwill and behavior. This attitude will increase our overall self-respect and self-discipline.

Discipline is an attribute that enhances our self-worth, self-respect, and self-dignity. Those who possess it have the potential to possess greatness. Those who lack the will of living a disciplined lifestyle have a greater chance of living with the inevitable and regrettable consequences. It is in our disciplined interest that we embrace the fact that "Anything I can Conceive, I can Achieve if I Believe."

Hilltop Thoughts:

- Backward planning enables us to plan for awards.
- Listening is an art. Some of us lack the creative ability to sculpture effective communication.
- The most valuable things in life are free, but some of life's choices can be costly.
- Reliable is a noteworthy title. In order to be recognized as such, we must demonstrate the ability to be trusted.
- Positive thinking is the anecdote to the epidemic of negative thoughts, actions, or behaviors.
- Positive people will support, inspire, and motivate others. Negative people will support, inspire, and motivate fear, doubt, and disbelief.
- Potential unveiled is synonymous with superpowers revealed.
- When we deposit prayers into our faith account, this prevents us from bouncing a check from our trials and tribulations account.
- Do not be content with the appetizers of success. We must be determined to feast on the smorgasbord of opportunities.
- Allow me to introduce myself. My name is Change, but my friends call me Opportunity.

RESPONSIBILITY, ACCOUNTABILITY

Train up a child in the way he should go: and
when he is old, he will not depart from it.

—Proverbs 22:6

We must understand that it is vital that we acquire the necessary skills to achieve our dreams, and some of the most prominent tools required to succeed in life is responsibility and accountability. The manifestation of responsibility and accountability in life is attributed to maturity and the ability to develop a clear and concise understanding of personal obligations and individual liability. These principles are significant to our personal and professional development, and each of us should institute the benefits of both into our collection of character strengths.

It is imperative that we fully comprehend that we can delegate authority but never responsibility. Being accountable in life distinguishes us from the oblivious. Our commitment to answerable behaviors enables us to make responsible decisions and be accountable for the outcome whether it be good, bad, or indifferent. An individual or group can be identified as responsible beginning with a concept to its completion, but we can only be identified as accountable if the assigned mission or task is either complete or incomplete.

Many of us are fully aware of the benefits of responsible conduct and behavior as an individual or as a leader, supervisor, or manager of assigned task(s), project(s), organization(s), or municipalities. Whenever we are acknowledged as the person responsible, we realize that we have an obligation to uphold and ensure timelines are met, documents are recorded, and expenses are covered. If any of the above tasks have been neglected someone has to be held accountable.

Through maturation and dedication to sustaining all that you have worked for to establish a good name enables you to commit to responsible behavior and character traits. Our abilities and conduct define our recognition by being trustworthy, dependable, and in alignment with the virtues of integrity. Being responsible allows you to learn from mistakes and be accountable for the cause and effect.

Responsibility and accountability define the importance of earning respect through conscious efforts of treating others the way you would like to be treated and honoring others by keeping your promises. When we engage in conversation, this allows others to interpret our strengths and weaknesses, the inability to uphold commitments instills a doubt cloud over your name, and a shady reputation is damaging to your credibility.

Throughout life, we will be presented with ethical dilemmas, and our choices and decisions to sustain our honor by being accountable for our personal choices, actions, and behaviors will instill trust in others that we are deserving of a good name and good reputation. If we were to look through our personal contacts list of family and friends, it is disturbing to realize that we each have a small percentage of family, friends, and associates that we can truly depend on as being responsible and accountable for their personal and professional responsibilities. Yes, we have some that meet the prerequisites, but we also have some that do not. You must take the necessary measures to ensure that if anyone scrolls across your name, whether it is in a contact list on a phone, business card, Facebook, or Instagram, when they see your name, they are confident that you are as credible as your word based upon the confidence you have instilled in them over the years or even as early as your initial impression.

If you borrow money from a family member or friend, embrace the importance of returning the money as promised. If you are loaned a tool to complete a project or a cooking dish to enjoy a meal, ensure you protect that item and return it with appreciation. If you are presented with a meal to take home in a dish that is expected to be returned, clean the dish thoroughly and place a gift such as chocolates or mints inside the dish as a token of appreciation for the hospitality when you return it. If you borrow a chain saw or lawn mower, return the item cleaner than you received it, and ensure you return it with a full tank of gas.

We must utilize responsible discretion with who and what we focus our attention on. Our social circles represent our societal goals. When you recognize that your ability to identify who has your best interest at heart, this demonstrates growth simply because "real recognizes real." Our circles are a direct reflection of what we love, appreciate, and stand for. When our companions are genuine, they will contribute to positive influences and inspirations. Our wisdom will guide us to surround ourselves with promising peers with responsible and accountable virtues. Our character strengths enable us to utilize creditable judgment and separate ourselves from the mediocre and position ourselves amongst thriving goal-oriented individuals because "Anything I can Conceive, I can Achieve if I Believe."

Hilltop Thoughts:

- Hesitation has the potential of being mistaken for procrastination.
- Scientific research has proven that you are defined as an amazing specimen.
- GPS is designed to assist us in arriving at our desired destination. Our conscious is also one of life's navigational tools.
- When we identify with our individual purpose, we will recognize the signatures of our identity.
- We must nourish our goals to allow our dreams to grow into healthy success.
- Reflections of life's memorable moments are choices that mirror our heart's image.
- We must free our mind from the torture chambers of ineptitude, inadequacy, and incapable thoughts.
- The strength of family is immeasurable. We have to stop measuring our sisters and brothers.
- Greet the stranger in your presence as if you are presenting a heartfelt present filled with the presence of kindness.
- Our thirst for success can only be quenched by the sweat of the struggle.

RÉSUMÉS VS. BUSINESS PLANS

And the Lord answered me and said, "Write the vision, and make it plain upon tables that he may run that readeth it."
—Habakkuk 2:2

Résumés are utilized to establish an initial impression of an individual's knowledge, skills, and capabilities. Prospective employers usually make their determination of the most qualified applicants based upon the information contained within the résumé. Your professional résumé is basically a documented sales pitch of what you bring to the table.

Business plans are strategic outlines for a proposed business that details a structured game plan illustrating the specifics in relation to potential consumer products or specialized services.

Résumés and business plans are the foundation of your occupational endeavors whether you are pursuing a job or starting a professional business. It really does not matter if you are a teenager in search of your first job or an adult attempting to land the job of your dreams. It is imperative that you provide the employer, financial lenders, or investors a definitive depiction of your potential greatness. Résumés paint the potential employer a picture of your occupational strengths and qualifications in addition to your personal and professional accomplishments.

First and foremost, we want the résumé to stand out. However, there are parameters to consider, such as size of the font, color, length, and fancy formatting. We want to gain the attention of the human resources recruiter by presenting a professional arrangement of your work-related proficiencies. There are various types of résumés to consider—for example, chronological, functional, combination, and targeted.

You must be able to determine which type of resume will best represent you in a manner that achieves your objectives of establishing the fact that your experience, skills, and capabilities are in alignment with what the prospective employer is looking for.

Chronological résumés illustrate your talents, experience, skills, and capabilities based upon your employment history in chronological order from the most recent to the beginning. This is an effective format for those with consistent work history especially if it corresponds with the prospective position you are applying for. Twelve to fifteen years should be a sufficient amount of history unless a previous occupation will clearly establish credibility through experience.

Functional résumés identify your professional skills, certifications, and overall occupational experience. The primary objective is to recognize your specializations and professional knowledge within this particular field of employment. The skills of your craft are highlighted as opposed to your history of employment. Utilizing this format allows you to take the focus off the lapses in employment.

Combination résumés are designed to recognize your knowledge, skills, and abilities in a chronological format of your occupational history. This résumé style allows you to illustrate your strengths and attributes as a professional. Focus on highlighting your most recent experience and accomplishments with consideration of the space constraints.

Targeted résumés are basically created to identify how your knowledge, skills, and abilities are correlated to the position of interest. You are physically prepared to serve in this position based upon your experience, capabilities, and education of the specified craft.

The overall objective is to ensure your résumé captivates the reader's interest enough to influence them into scheduling you for an interview. It is imperative that you clearly define yourself in a manner that gives your résumé the power to open doors or stimulate enough interest to capture an interview.

Dos and don'ts are important when writing a resume. Let's discuss a few.

Do your research. Do your best to provide the employer the best product résumé possible. Do what is necessary to enable you the opportunity to be interviewed for the position of interest.

Don't lie. Definitely, don't be lazy and submit a generic résumé. Don't forget to let someone else proofread your résumé, and don't overdo it with fancy colors or pictures or extravagant font.

Always remember that your résumé is your opportunity spokesperson, and you must prepare it with character, confidence, and class. Your résumé serves as a segue to catapult you from unemployment to employment with benefits and, most importantly, compensation.

Résumés save employers valuable time by allowing them to discern between prospective competitors, so it is important that your résumé clearly illustrates your value, strengths, and capabilities.

Now let's discuss the benefits or professional business plans. Business plans provide entrepreneurs a structured template of a business proposal that will assist them in their endeavors of acquiring financial assistance through loans or investors. Financial institutions will not finance your dreams based upon good ideas or intentions. We must be able to clearly illustrate a business model that outlines a successful formula that will result in net profits. Your ability to identify a road map to prospective lenders or investors validates your passion, commitment, and business savviness. Thorough research is essential. We must consider the business industry and specific market competition. The underlying principle behind the creation of a business plan is a strategic outline of expectations and potential growth.

Google is a tremendous tool that will aid and assist you with developing a strong résumé or business plan. Utilize every resource available to enable you to develop the best product possible. Each of these tools are designed to increase opportunities and prosperity, and it is vital that we are acutely aware of the advantages associated with both. The résumé is designed to open doors to allow you to work for a quality organization. The business plan is designed to allow you to open the doors for others to work for a quality organization.

Dependent upon your upbringing and mentorship, you will be inspired to pursue employment working for others, or you will be encouraged to create opportunities for others by starting your own business. Nevertheless, your knowledge of both will greatly enhance your opportunities to achieve greatness because "Anything I can Conceive, I can Achieve if I Believe."

Hilltop Thoughts:

- The hands of time are manicured by memorable moments.
- We, as individuals, families, and a nation, have to recognize, support, and commit to the ideation of a family reunion.
- May your response to the unknown challenges be acknowledged by your unknown strengths.
- Calculated steps on divided paths of reasoning will increase our percentage of the sum total of our success.
- Profitable results require laborious planning.
- When we measure our choices, we are able to make sound decisions.
- We must upgrade our aspirations of elevation from "coach doubt" to "first class faith."
- Every day is a picture of life. Smile for the human cameras.
- Victorious finish lines are crossed by strides of preparation.
- Reading increases the opportunity of being ready.

POSITIVE ATTITUDE VS. NEGATIVE ATTITUDE

Humble yourselves in the sight of the Lord, and he shall lift you up.
—James 4:10

Positivity aligns our thoughts, actions, and behaviors in a favorable position as opposed to the unfortunates associated with a negative attitude. A positive attitude promotes productive responses and reactions to the everyday challenges we encounter. Challenges are inevitable throughout life, and how we interpret them will dictate how we respond to them. Some of us face similar and sometimes identical trials. How we respond is attributed to our overall attitude. I was once introduced to a story about positive and negative attitudes that has provided me a new outlook on how to approach some of life's uncontrollable circumstances. I will do my best to describe it in a manner that allows you to decide what your approach would be like. Hopefully we can adopt new and improved approaches to how we respond to unfavorable predicaments.

As a lawyer walked out of his home and approached his vehicle, he noticed that he had a flat tire. He immediately dropped his brief case on the ground, threw his hands in the air, and began to exercise his freedom of speech, which involved multiple expletives. He then proceeded to kick the tire and rampage about the scene while reminding himself that "life sucks." This was only the beginning of his terrible day. Well it just so happens that down the street, a doctor walked out of his home. As he approached his vehicle, he noticed that he had a flat tire. He immediately thought to himself, *I have a four-way lug wrench with a jack and a spare tire in the trunk. I should be able to replace this tire and be on my way in fifteen to twenty minutes and still have a blessed day.* Each of these gentlemen faced similar circumstances with completely opposite reactions.

We have choices in how we choose to respond to unforeseen predicaments. Our willingness to adopt new approaches will greatly enhance our inner strength and our overall health. Stress is medically documented as a silent killer, and undue stress can be avoided through our ability to control our responses to everyday difficulties and dilemmas. Our ability to focus on the blessings in life as opposed to, placing emphasis on the complicated circumstances will enhance our mental state of being. Our ability to realize that "tough times never last, tough people do" will place us in a more favorable position of strength instead of a position of pity or depression.

Our personal and professional attitude is a direct reflection of our character, and they should both coincide with the spirit of the heart. We must strive to fully grasp the importance of realizing that "life is 10 percent what happens to you and 90 percent how you react to it" (Charles R. Swindell). Our responses are representative of our self-control as well as our attitude. Regardless of how dreadful the circumstances, we must possess the ability to respond responsibly in a manner that represents productive accountability. Negative thoughts, decisions, responses, and behaviors result in negative consequences. Positive thoughts, decisions, responses, and behaviors result in positive consequences. Our attitude plays an instrumental role in our choices based upon how well we will respond to good, bad, or indifferent conditions. Calm, cool, and collective demeanors are representative of the disciplined conduct that we should strive to embody as we manifest positive consequences.

Negative views, opinions, and behaviors produce negative feelings associated with disappointment, resentment, frustration, anger, etc. Negativity contributes to stress, anxiety, and tension, which are all connected to heart disease, heart attacks, and strokes. Pessimistic mindsets are directly responsible for unhealthy, unproductive, and unhappy lifestyles.

Positive views, opinions, and behaviors produce positive feelings associated with goals, achievements, resolutions, gratitude, and blessings. Positivity contributes to optimism, hope, and confidence.

Our mental discipline contributes to our overall ability to embrace the significance of a positive attitude versus negative attitude. Disappointment, sadness, frustration are natural feelings, but they are also controllable feelings that can be superseded by faith, hope, and determination. Our attitudes will vary according to our social and economic status, our personal and professional goals, education, skills, and most importantly our relationship with GOD.

Our lives are signified by three inscriptions on our tombstones: our date of arrival, our date of departure, and the dash in the middle. That dash is the most significant because it represents what we embodied in life—meaning, the good, the bad, and everything else in the middle. Our attitudes and behaviors are something that many people will reminisce about once they come together as family and friends to celebrate our life once we are deceased. Many pastors are placed in awkward situations when requested to perform the services for individuals who had negative attitudes, influences, and lifestyles. Our goals should include providing the pastor the best obituary possible as opposed to placing the pastor in an ethical dilemma, causing them to present false truths to appease their family and friends. Our beliefs, actions, and behaviors are what will be illustrated within our obituaries. Positive thoughts, decisions, responses, and behaviors result in positive consequences, which will result in the pastor being able to communicate the blessings of your dash and allow them to illustrate your greatness and positive contributions to society, friends, and family. The blessings of a positive attitude are boundless because "Anything I can Conceive, I can Achieve if I Believe."

Hilltop Thoughts:

- A breath of fresh air can be inhaled or exhaled dependent upon the conditions of the air.
- Typical responses are typically not received with enthusiasm.
- Teamwork is like a bag of ice cubes. Together they remain cool, isolated they meltdown.
- Three course meal of life: age one to twenty-five, appetizer; twenty-five to fifty, main course; fifty plus, dessert.
- We have a choice in life to be pushed or pulled or to push or pull others.
- Family is like fabric woven together that interlocks the threads to strengthen the complete canvas.
- Undeveloped goals are symbolic of unreleased opportunities.
- Our ancestors possessed the courage to travel the unpaved paths so that our journeys will not involve the same detours.
- Our respect for the less fortunate enables us to respect our fortunes.
- We will embrace our fruits by supporting our branches based upon the strength of our roots.

PURPOSE

*To everything, there is a season and a time to
every purpose under the heaven.*

—Ecclesiastes 3:1

Allow me to remind you that every single person blessed with the ability to breathe life since birth has a purpose on this earth. Many of us struggle with the fact that our mere existence is a miracle. Our presence is a gift to our loved ones from the very day we were delivered from the womb to the inevitable day we are laid to rest in our tomb. Our ability to embrace the "dash" and recognize qualities associated with our purpose will elevate our motivation and desires to increase our efforts to make a difference.

Each of us face personal and professional challenges, but our purpose is not defined by our misfortunes. Our introduction to a sense of purpose allows us to recognize how we respond to less fortunate circumstances. Our ability to face adversity with confidence is attributed to our commitment to the belief that we will not be defeated. Our strength and convictions prevent us from throwing in the towel. Many of us who have been challenged by the circumstances connected with poverty, injustice, racism, inequality, or discrimination understand the significance of identifying problems and responding with solutions. Unfortunately, some of our solutions are not considered the most appropriate.

As responsible citizens within the community, it is necessary to explore and research the available resources that are designed to address life-challenging circumstances through programs of assistance, education, and inspiration. Our willingness to pursue measures that will aid and assist others will also allow us to increase through selfless service. Personal growth is attributed to identifying with positive characteristics, creative thinking, and optimism. Our individual efforts to increase our opportunities are essential elements that will provide us the means to meet community aspirations.

A productive mindset combined with a desire for self-development evolves into a self-fulfilling purpose. Our motivations can be attributed to our willingness to engage in inspirational literature pertaining to goals, dreams, and success. Personal enhancement videos, podcasts and audio books can be instrumental in an individual's quest for personal development. Proven methods support models of emulation. Motivational speakers encourage us to pursue greatness in the same manner. Bottom line: Success magnetizes admiration. Our ability to embrace the realness of opportunities and commitments enable us to take the appropriate measures to identify goal-driven plans.

Our motivation and determination are reflections of our mental discipline, strength, and focus. In order for greatness to materialize, we have to implement a plan of action. A structured game plan resembles increased chances of accomplishment as opposed to driving blind with the intent of wandering upon wholesome opportunities.

When we lose interest, we must remind ourselves what our motives are. When our drive diminishes, we must refuel the fire with mental explanations of purpose. When we allow doubt to invade our concentration, we must root out the uncertainties and replace them with faith-based incentives.

Our admiration for another person's abilities and achievements should inspire us to scrutinize their foundation of accomplishments. When we celebrate the boxing heavyweight champion of the world, we have to consider how many times they actually sparred in the ring, how many hours of speed bag, heavy bag, jumping rope, shadow boxing, weight training, and running they put in.

When we celebrate an NBA champion of the world, we have to consider how many suicides, carioca, and scrimmages have they run, ball handling and dribbling exercises performed, how many free throws, jumpers, three-pointers they have taken in preparation for the game's winning shot. These champion's abilities and achievements are evidenced by their motivation to achieve their personal and professional goals.

When we celebrate a defense attorney winning a case against the prosecuting district attorney, we have to consider their motivation to prepare for the opportunity to represent their client. Their preparation enables them to increase their overall understanding of the case better than their opponent. This allows them to control the courtroom. Their preparation instills confidence in the client, jury, and the judge.

Our motivation must resemble that of a professional athlete, journeyman, or scholar determined to cross the finish line, certification, or graduation. Our motivation must be unwavering throughout our expedition to greatness. Professional achievers possess a strong sense of mental strength, attributing to the will to learn, grow, and achieve greatness. Our personal drive thrives on consistency. The more active and aggressive we are in pursuit of our endeavors, the more evident our accomplishments will be revealed. Success is not a location, position, or accomplishment. Success is encompassed by the trials, tribulations, and roads traveled to achieve our personal and professional goals.

Our strength is portrayed by our feats and our ability to bounce back after failing. Our failures contribute to our greatness through education, experience, and edification of how not to do things. We must allow failure to illuminate our shortcomings to expose our gifts. Our quest to elevate mentally, physically, and financially is based upon our personal drive, motivation, and execution.

The gift of motivation combined with relentless purpose is not afforded to everyone, but those who possess these prosperous traits are inclined to excel in all aspects of life. Our personal drive is defined by our commitment to our individual purpose. The overall intensity that we invest into our self-development will result in accomplishments. Personal goals achieved result in a sense of personal gratification, which results in self-confidence, which results in personal and professional growth.

We are capable of achieving daily greatness through altruistic ventures and compassion-related objectives. The harder we grind, the stronger our mind works to sustain a relentless mentality. Our ability to cultivate a mindset of strength through action allows us to give back to society through productive measures and purposeful contributions. When we can capitalize on the significance of aiding and assisting others, the benefits fall into the category that is best described as blessings. Personal and professional motivation personifies our character and enhances our physical and mental stamina. Our inexorable efforts to grow must be nourished with a mindset to make a difference.

The day you arrive on this earth will be celebrated with cakes and candles. The day you depart this earth will be celebrated with flowers and tears. The dash in the middle of those dates should be celebrated with purpose. The length of the dash does not define the person, but the purpose of your dash has the ability to inspire greatness. Live your dash with Faith, Hope, Prosperity, and Purpose because "Anything I can Conceive, I can Achieve if I Believe."

Hilltop Thoughts:

- The depth of the phrase captures the warmth of the heart.
- Supernatural powers are the products of supernatural faith.
- Some of the most profound are responsible for what they have found in others.
- Forward-thinking enables us to fall forward.
- The quest of elevation requires dedication to the transformation.
- Our ability to assemble a puzzle based upon the presented photo reassures us that if we present ourselves with a clear picture of our goals, we can assemble a puzzle of hope. Hint: Establish your borders first, and your puzzle will grow into the vision.
- Being prepared is guaranteed when you preprayer.
- Respectful options provide us alternatives to disrespectful opinions.
- Fortunately, it is irrelevant how we fell; but it is vital that we know how to get up.
- We must strive to formulate letters into words into sentences into paragraphs into our stories of our library of abilities.

MY BROTHER'S KEEPER

Behold, how good and how pleasant it is for
brethren to dwell together in unity.

—Psalms 133:1

The evolution of development, progress, and growth is attributed to role models, advisors, and mentors. As aspiring young men, we are dependent upon the knowledge, skills, and abilities of our elders to acquire the necessary tools to sustain ourselves throughout life. This is why we must embrace the importance of our responsibilities to serve as "My Brother's Keeper." We have a responsibility to challenge our youth through motivation, education, and empowerment. We must stand firm in our beliefs and uphold our ethics, values, virtues as the pillars of our family, community, and society.

During the year of 2001, I was raised to the sublime degree of a Master Mason, which was soon followed by the achievement of traveling up the York Rite side of the House to the Purple, Red and Black House, eventually allowing me to cross the hot sands of the Desert to the Ancient Egyptian Arabic Order Nobles Mystic Shrine. My affiliation with these organizations has taught me the principles of the Fatherhood of GOD and the Brotherhood of Men. I embarked upon an obligation to walk upright before Man and GOD, and I will uphold that commitment until the day my Brothers in arms fold the American flag over my casket.

The demonstration of good, orderly conduct, self-discipline, and self-respect are commendable traits that should be emulated by each of us in our efforts to epitomize the character traits of responsible human beings. Children, adolescents, and young adults imitate, emulate, and attempt to identify with what they witness from family members, acquaintances, community leaders, and celebrities. Responsible and accountable behaviors involve the commitment of setting a good example by conducting ourselves accordingly. The sooner we grasp the fact that we truly possess the ability to influence good, bad, or evil impressions upon our youth's actions, responses, and behaviors, the sooner we will be able to identify the appropriate measures to implement positive contributions through productive choices. It is critically important that we strive to influence and develop positive attitudes and behaviors by demonstrating positive attitudes and behaviors, which is basically attributed to our positive mindset and behavioral discipline. Our youth are constantly seeking guidance and approval, either subtly or overtly, and we must be conscious of the ques in efforts of responding appropriately whenever possible. Due to the inevitable challenges associated with our youth, ranging from peer pressure, academics, social, personal, and emotional events, we have to personify and encourage psychological strength through positivity and perseverance.

As "My Brother's Keeper," our problem-solving skills must be imaginative and absolute. We have to prepare ourselves to respond to the most volatile circumstances and disgusting emotional events ranging from bullying, homicides, physical and/or sexual abuse. Our mental stamina will allow us to counsel, mentor, and facilitate conversations in a manner that is circumstantially conducive based solely on the fact that we genuinely care about our brothers.

As "My Brother's Keeper," we have to promote the benefits associated with the skill of listening. Our communication tools are best utilized when we implement the sender-receiver-feedback method to ensure both parties' messages are delivered and received as intended and interpreted with complete understanding.

Our ability to communicate with a sincere sense of concern and compassion demonstrates our consideration for others and will open dialogue, which increases the opportunity to establish trust, which will strengthen the personal relationship. Once we have established a mutual connection of trust, we can focus on their short-term, mid-term, and long-term goals. It is imperative that we utilize effective communication to convince our youth to identify, illustrate, and implement a game plan to achieve their personal and professional goals through strategic aspirations.

As "My Brother's Keeper," we must be willing to dedicate time, energy, and a personal commitment to the betterment of our youth through selfless service and cognizant examples of creditable conduct in public and private surroundings. We cannot and should not promote the importance of living and walking a straight line in the presence of others and, in veiled circumstances, participate in activities that can be questioned or even perceived as immoral or dishonorable. Our communities and society, as a whole, have suffered at the hands of certain individuals serving in the capacity of public servants and community leaders whose underlying intent was only to benefit by unscrupulous means of financial, ethical, criminal, and sexual misconduct at the expense of naive believers in a greater cause, community, and country. They may have initially endeavored to make a difference, but their moral compasses were swayed by temptation and unprincipled behaviors. We have a moral obligation to uphold and support the efforts of those who have walked the paths of the freedom fighters, abolitionist, civil rights activists who dedicated their lives to provide a better life for the oppressed.

As "My Brother's Keeper," remember this important acronym ICE-UP: Inspire, Coach, Encourage, Uplift, and most importantly, Pray for our brothers. Now is the time to ask yourself, "Am I My Brother's keeper?" This is not a rhetorical question. We must be willing to answer this question with an honest response and conduct ourselves accordingly. Our willingness to serve in the capacity of a difference maker will enable our brothers to achieve their dreams because "Anything I can Conceive, I can Achieve if I Believe."

Hilltop Thoughts:

- My strengths shall not be measured by mirrors or pounds but by morals, values, and ethics.
- I am capable…
- The risk versus reward spectrum involves decisions, choices, and consequences.
- Dehydrated growth performance can be hydrated with goals, benchmarks, and purpose-driven planning.
- When the enemy has your back against the wall, mentally transform the wall into a bridge, and work toward crossing it together.
- To mastermind, a master plan in life requires the willingness to mind the master of life.
- Lessons are learned when we learn to lessen the unnecessaries.
- Program your mind to feed the positive and starve the negative.
- Mental chains harness greatness. Unleash your brilliance.

ADDICTION

Without question, the perils of addiction have crippled dreams, aspirations, opportunities, goals, objectives, and hopes. The Hilltop has suffered some of the worst afflictions associated with addiction. Like many Hilltops across the United States of Addiction, our resilience has prevailed. Addiction is a complicated disease attributed to a chronic dysfunction within the brain and body that creates cravings for substances or behaviors without regard for consequences or complications involved.

My introduction to alcohol and illegal substances did not include a warning label. What it did include was broken promises, heartache, loss of self-respect, loss of trust, pain, tears, and humiliation—just to name a few. Many of us who chose/choose to engage in the life of recreational activities involving drugs and alcohol do not realize that this choice has the propensity to develop into terminal addiction(s). It is not uncommon that those that delve into experimenting with the unknown assumes the philosophy of a "not me" attitude rarely ever will an individual accept the fact that they are susceptible to the vices of addiction. I am here to share a cold-hearted fact, which is addiction does not discriminate. The demons associated with addiction are strategic, manipulative, persuasive, unscru-pulous, and deceptive. Addiction is the devil that walketh like a lion.

> Be sober, be vigilant; because your adversary
> the devil, as a roaring lion, walketh about, seek-
> ing whom he may devour. (1 Peter 5:8)

My struggles have paralleled many. In comparison to others, my dependence only scratched the surface of some people battling the demons of addiction. When I think back to my teenage years of ven-turing out to engage with others to realize an altered reality to mask my insecurities, pain, and uncertainties with a false sense of accep-tance of my circumstances relating to every facet of my life, I realize the truths in the statement my mentor in sobriety shared with me: "Everything happens for a reason or with reason." A child faced with challenges tends to seek refuge in many forms whether it be healthy or unhealthy, positive or negative, legal or illegal. My response to the inevitable challenges of life completely changed my life in many forms. My personal involvement with drugs and alcohol attributes to my troubled youth, which evolved into patterns of misconduct and criminal mischief as a young adult.

Many will not understand the following statement, but my addiction to drugs and alcohol is something I treasure because of the lessons and experiences that have allowed me to evolve into a man of gratitude. The misfortunes, calamities, and disappointments I expe-rienced during my life of addiction have allowed me to embrace the importance of my individual purpose and serenity.

One weekend when I was in the eighth grade at Hunt Junior High School, my close friend came to my house to visit, and some-how we started discussing how his older brother had a friend that lived right down the street from where I lived, and he had some weed growing in his backyard. Well we decided to help ourselves to some of his newly grown product. We snuck into his backyard, and we each grabbed several plants in both hands and bolted back to my house. We went into my garage and devised a plan to have one of our older friends dry out and prepare the plants so we could smoke the weed. So we put all of the plants into a big, brown paper bag and headed to our friend's house. He said it would take several days to dry out. Several days passed, and he brought the weed to school and gave it to us. We were definitely not impressed with the final product. It appeared to have shrunk quite a bit, and it was pure shake. None of that really mattered, we were just happy to have our own weed to do whatever we wanted to do with it. Once he gave me the weed, my friend and I decided that we would split it up later, and I would hold on to it for the time being.

Well it just so happens the day prior, we had a substitute teacher in our English class. When the regular teacher returned, I was identified as being insubordinate with the substitute, so I was required to report to the principal's office. The principal explained to me that my pattern of misconduct would not be tolerated. If I got into any more trouble, I would get suspended from school. Upon completion of my verbal reprimand, the principal told me to wait in the lobby for the remainder of the period and then proceed to my next class. Well as I was waiting in the office lobby, I watched the principal leave his office and leave my file on his desk with all of my information, including my negative reports of conduct. I came up with a brilliant plan that if I stole my file from his office, he could not determine how much trouble I had been in, and he would not be able to suspend me if I was to get into trouble again. I told the secretary I left my wallet in the principal's office. She told me to go into the office and retrieve it. I went into the office and grabbed my file from his desk and placed it inside my shirt and walked back out into the lobby and sat down for the remainder of the period. Once the bell rang, I left the office and proceeded to my next class, which was physical education. Well while I was in PE, the principal walked in the gym and requested to see me and the PE instructor, Mr. Boyd. They asked me several times to open my gym locker, and I persisted to tell them that I could not remember the combination to my lock, but they were persistent. After about thirty minutes of attempting to coerce me into opening the lock, they told me that they will cut the lock if necessary, so I banged my fist on the bench and yelled out with a broken voice, "I'm tired of playing games." My T-Town Crew

Brothers still clown and mock me for saying that. Anyways, I finally proceeded to open the combination lock. Once I unlocked the lock, I attempted to reach inside the locker, but the principal moved me to the side, reached inside the locker, and grabbed my personal file. As he pulled my white painter pants and white velour sweater out of the locker, he then grabbed my white crayon shoes with the orange bottoms, and inside of the shoes was a bag containing 8.8 grams of weed from the guy down the street. At that point, I was escorted back to the principal's office, and the interrogation began.

The principal notified the Tacoma Police Department. Once the police officer arrived, he began grilling me up and down as to where I got the weed. I told them that I found it on a roller-coaster ride at the Puyallup Fair, and I stuck to that story all the way up until the officer dropped me off at my Aunt Debbie's house because my parents were not at home. They were at work, and they had no way of contacting them. I was suspended from school and kicked off of the football team. News travels fast, and everybody knew I was not a snitch. Everybody now knew I got high. Both of these attributes worked to my advantage amongst my friends at school and on Hilltop. This incident contributed to my lifestyle and attraction to misconduct and association with drugs and alcohol.

My initial contact with drugs and alcohol was innocent through curiosity and obliviousness to the long-term effects. Everybody who is personally familiar with this disease has their own individual story—some similar to mine, some more extreme. In the end, any life that involves addiction is vexing and dysfunctional. Unfortunately, our initial encounter with drugs and/or alcohol is usually inviting and alluring. What many of us fail to realize is that what appears to be an innocent recreational introduction can result in tragedy, misfortune, and the obliteration of families and friendships.

Addiction to drugs and alcohol can affect us in so many different ways that it is truly immeasurable. We must continue to inform the nonbelievers that addiction does not discriminate. According to historical data, without rebuttal, America has a record of discrimination when dealing with drug-related crimes.

According to case studies, African Americans who engage in a life of drugs are three times more likely to be arrested by authorities than others. The fact remains that throughout society, we are faced with drug-related charges, which contributes to the statistics of the significant disparities in numbers of drug offenses in relation to minorities. I share this information not to illuminate the misfortunes of minorities but more importantly to inform everyone of the dangers involved with engaging in this lifestyle, most especially when you take into consideration that the consequences are amplified if your complexion is of a darker hue.

We, as productive citizens in society, must make a conscious effort to educate our youth and eliminate the desires associated with the experimentation of drugs and alcohol as opposed to glorifying this lifestyle through music, peer pressure, and negative influences. It is imperative that we expose how addiction impacts our society to include domestic violence, child abuse, homelessness, incarceration, poverty, health concerns, mental challenges, financial burdens, violent crimes, abandonment, sexual crimes, unemployment, etc.

Addiction distresses, damages, destroys, and kills members of our families throughout America every single day. Regrettably, even with education, information, and motivation, addiction still continues to plague our country at an alarming rate. I would like to challenge every responsible person in a position to make a difference to utilize their individual skill sets to influence family and friends to realize and embrace the advantages and opportunities associated with abstinence.

I would like to take a pause for the cause for a moment. Yes, I understand and agree with the fact that some people can engage in the use of alcohol and marijuana without becoming addicted and also sustain a responsible lifestyle without negative consequences. For the other 90 percent of us who graduated from occasional interactions with these socially accepted substances to wake and bake and a need for a hair off the dog that bit 'em, I would like to share some inspirational information that is designed to encourage those who have fallen victim to the perils of addiction.

I believe that there are several measures that people can take to address and conquer the demons of addiction. Even though there are a vast number of creative methods or techniques utilized to achieve sobriety, whatever works for that particular individual should be supported and reinforced on a continual basis.

First and foremost, we must realize the importance of embracing the blessings from the Grand Architect Of The Universe, "GOD." I sincerely believe that "My story is His Glory." Once I came to terms with the Bible verse, "I can do all things through Christ which strengthen me" (Philippians 4:13), I was transformed into a believer that understood that my addiction was smaller than my GOD. My addiction was not as important to me as my GOD. My addiction did not deserve as much attention as my GOD. I finally came to realize that it was time for my addiction to bow down to my GOD. My Lord and Savior has bestowed upon me blessings, opportunities, faith, strength, and wisdom not to exclude one of my most valued attributes—that being gratitude. I give all glory to GOD for allowing me to sustain my sobriety, utilizing unconventional but proven methods through unfiltered faith and the laws of attraction.

Ask yourself a reasonable question: "Have you been involved in multiple alcohol-related incidents or drug related incidents that resulted in negative consequences?" If the answer is yes, I challenge you to reevaluate your relationship with drugs and alcohol.

Self-evaluation: We know ourselves better than anybody. The most critical factor in a self-analysis is honesty. When we ask ourselves the tough questions pertaining to drugs and alcohol and answer them with unequivocal honesty, then we are on a productive path to recovery.

Implementing change: Our understanding of the importance of change in relation to people, places, and things will improve our chances of sustaining our sobriety if we are able to implement the appropriate changes to our current lifestyle and accept the positive consequences associated with change.

Identify with your truth: I am battling addiction, but I am blessed. I am disappointed in my lifestyle choices, but I am capable of achieving greatness. I am not living to my full potential, but I can do anything and become anything I want to be.

Cognitive behavioral therapy: This is a psychosocial intervention designed to enhance mental stamina and target addictive behaviors through coping mechanisms and strategic methods of addressing dysfunctional behaviors.

The Pain is temporary: Withdrawals, sickness, and illness associated with quitting can be painful, but the pain is temporary. We are all familiar with the statement of "what does not kill you will make you stronger." Yes, it will be difficult once we accept the fact that getting clean and sober is not easy, because if it were, anybody could do it. Keep the faith and always remember that once we get through the pain, the joy of being back in control of your life is indescribable.

Twelve-step programs: The twelve steps originated with Alcoholics Anonymous in efforts of overcoming the addiction to alcohol. Over the years, a vast number of twelve-step programs have been created to address various forms of addiction. They are based upon principles designed to provide a path to sobriety. They only work if you work the steps.

Addiction comes in many forms, our willingness to face it head on with faith and conviction will allow us to conquer it with positive consequences. Once we are able to address and control our disease, I challenge you to reach out and assist others in their battles with these disguised demons of destruction. I believe that we can be part of the problem or part of the solution. Hilltop has enough problems; it would be nice to witness the positive consequences of our solutions.

Throughout life, we utilize different motivations to move us in the right direction. I personally have a list of five, but it was not until I jeopardized them that I was able to put them into proper perspective. Aside from my wife, Aprile, my brother, Kenny, is my best friend. Before, during, and after my military career, Kenny has held me in the highest regard and has done everything to help me sustain my prestigious career to include fulfilling the duty as the designated driver whenever we were out drinking together until one day when my brother and I were out making random visits, and he was pulled over while driving my rental car, and I was passed out and drunk in the back seat. Well he was hauled off to jail, and the rental car was towed back to Sea-Tac Airport. The next day while visiting family, I was discussing bailing out my brother from jail. During the conversation with a couple of my bros, Robert and Lionel, I was expressing how upset I was for letting Kenny drive. Robert stated that Kenny would not have had it any other way and that Kenny would do anything for me, and he definitely would not have allowed me to jeopardize my career. That was when Lionel intervened with his divine wisdom in which he asked us a question that I view as a significant emotional event in my life. Lionel asked, "What is more important, TC's job or KC's freedom?" That question was a wake-up call for me. It was the last time I have ever placed my brother in a compromising position. It also inspired my motivational virtues in life to this day.

1. I will not jeopardize my relationship with God.
2. I will not jeopardize my Family.
3. I will not jeopardize my Freedom.
4. I will not jeopardize my Safety.
5. I will not jeopardize my Health.

I treasure my sobriety with unparalleled respect, and I understand that I will never walk across a sobriety stage to receive a sobriety diploma. I can, will, and do celebrate every single evening that I lay my head on my pillow, knowing that I have lived another clean and sober day. I believe it is a privilege to have been provided a second chance by the GAOTU to make a difference through my actions as opposed to my words because "Anything I can Conceive, I can Achieve if I Believe."

Hilltop Thoughts:

- Blessings tend to disguise themselves as weapons formed against you.
- Estimate the value of your greatness by the price you are willing to pay to achieve it.
- Our ability to forgive our past mistakes will provide stability in building our future achievements.
- Confidence is our ability to confide our private thoughts into personal beliefs into public existence.
- Self-fulfilling prophecy: expectations that increase the probability of the predicted event.
- Never accept the thought that certain shoes are too big to fill. Accept the challenge of growing into them.
- Lester Hayes used Stick-Em glue to catch footballs. Dip your goals in superglue, and catch your dreams.
- Personal aspirations require motivation, determination, and perspiration.
- Entitlement endangers productive perspectives.
- Our ability to demonstrate professional obedience is a direct reflection of our ability to lead professionally.

PRISON, POLITICS, POWER

Peter, therefore, was kept in prison: but prayer was made without ceasing of the church unto GOD for him.

—Acts 12:5

For GOD hath not given us the spirit of fear but of power and of love and of a sound mind.

—2 Timothy 1:7

Our society is a formulation of individuals interacting to achieve their personal and professional objectives to meet their individual and social needs. Unmistakably, the utilization of prisons, politics, and power has tremendously influenced our economic, social, and industrial infrastructure.

By the grace of GOD, most of us have evaded the tentacles of the prison system that has sucked millions of our young men and women into the cells of hell. Our prison population has increased in astronomical numbers at an alarming rate of over 500 percent in recent years. One in five prisoners worldwide are essentially incarcerated within the United States of America. It is estimated that there are in excess of 2.1 million prisoners in the US alone. The unfortunates associated with mass incarceration is horrendous and indescribable and heart-wrenching when we look at how this impacts our society's inmates. America should take a stronger stance against the pitfalls of our prison systems. When we take into consideration all of the injustices linked to overcrowding, inadequate housing, health and welfare risks, insufficient rehabilitative programs, counseling, limited education, and recreational opportunities, the absence of public support for increased measures to improve the current circumstance will enable the inevitable onslaught of calamities.

I would like to take a moment to explain that I do not believe our prisoners are entitled to some of the luxuries associated with freedom, most especially if they have violated a child, senior citizen, or any other senseless crime. They should definitely be treated humanely in every aspect of the meaning. I believe every prisoner's circumstances are different and should not be afforded equal privileges, but they should be granted rewards based upon an organized merit system of conduct and accomplishments. Our prisoners are being inadvertently punished in addition to their sentence without a sincere intent of rehabilitation or concentrated efforts to promote undisputable measures of safety for the inmates. According to chronological disciplinary data, prison records substantiate that we have an ever-present problem with violence, sexual assaults, substance abuse, and various other crimes within these institutions. Crimes committed within these institutions should be dealt with accordingly to discourage misconduct and violations of governing laws within the penal system. With all that being said, privileges should be utilized as an incentive program that promotes education, socialization, communication, and responsible conduct. The utilization of incentive programs increases the potential to reintegrate our inmates successfully into society with the propensity to minimize the magnitudes associated with recidivism.

In addition to all of the injustices associated within our penal institutions, we are also facing an influx of profit for prison incentives throughout our nation. Political motivations are "a" if not "the" driving force behind the increase of private prisons. Ever since the inception of prisons across the United States of prosperity, there has always been room for a great deal of improvement in relation to therapeutic disciplinary treatment. Regrettably, our society has not taken enough measures in regard to the public interest of minimizing the atrocities occurring day to day within our penal systems. It is apparent that not enough has been done to force our legislative systems to address the unbearable conditions that exists in a vast amount of our prisons. Our country has placed emphasis on toughening laws on crimes. The most prominent crusade was the "War on Drugs." This campaign is responsible for overcrowding and increasing the overall prison population in the United States. Undeniably, the systemic racial disparities are substantiated through our criminal justice system's sentencing statistics. People of color have a higher percentage of prison convictions per capita to include extensive sentences in comparison to our White brothers and sisters.

With all of these facts, statistics, realities, and evidence, our nation, as a whole, has not embraced the seriousness of this ever-present problem that is snowballing out of control. Our overall lack of involvement in political interest consequently contributes to the dismantling of our families. We, as individuals, communities, and society, do not have to continue to contribute to this abyss of our men and women by placing ourselves in compromising positions. We have to realize that there are good teachers that educate our children and bad teachers that violate our children. There are good firemen that risk their lives in fires and bad firemen that are guilty of arson. There are good doctors that perform miracle surgeries and bad doctors guilty of malpractice. There are good priests that spread the word of GOD and bad priests guilty of molesting children. There are good cops that protect and serve our nation with the utmost respect for law and justice and bad cops guilty of police brutality and shooting unarmed suspects. There are good judges that abide by ethical principles and judicial integrity, and there are bad judges responsible for immoral injustice. I strongly believe in not painting an entire race, religion, or occupational force with a biased brush of guilt based upon the behaviors of the bad apples. This does not excuse the fact that African Americans have suffered some of the most heinous acts of cowardice crimes at the hands of unscrupulous criminals with badges.

The unaccountable actions of certain police officers have deteriorated the confidence, public trust, and community relations. The police department, as a whole, has a professional obligation to earn and uphold the respect and trust of the citizens within their communities, and this can only be achieved by admonishing those officers that commit crimes against local citizens. We most certainly cannot exempt the individuals that are aware of their colleague's inappropriate conduct, involvement, actions, or indiscretions. Failure to communicate to superiors or authorities the knowledge of a crime, inappropriate behavior, or injustice is unacceptable and should not be practiced throughout police departments or penal institutions. We have a moral and ethical obligation not to condone or participate in any activity that can be considered unjust to an individual regardless of their race, religion, sexual preference, gender, origin, etc. just to preserve their loyalty to an oath of silence commonly referred to as the "Blue Wall of Silence," "Blue Shield," or "Code Blue." This mentality of loyalty will exist for as long as the Blue Shield is promoted and/or protected. Police academies across our nation should instill in training cadets the importance of upholding justice, first and foremost, above fraternal obligations especially when it comes to unwarranted shootings or unnecessary acts of violence committed against our country's citizens. Until our justice system elevates the seriousness of unjustified deaths of unarmed suspects, this epidemic will continue to exist, along with the preservation of the "I was in fear for my life" mendacious justification. America, as a whole, must adopt proactive measures to alleviate continued acts of violence against our citizens of color. The good cops across our nation should be leading at the tip of the spear of the rank and the file to demonstrate a sincere commitment to breaking the chains of injustice, corruption, and unethical behaviors. It is apparent that until our good police officers throughout our police departments can influence action to diminish the immoralities that exist across our nation, our citizens will remain targets, victims, and casualties of injustice.

We, as responsible citizens, must also take an active role in policing our children and ourselves within our communities. "It takes a village" is not just a proverb or cliché, it is a proven method of collective efforts designed to sustain discipline and accountability within our communities. We must inspire our children to demonstrate a sense of respect for not only family members but also neighbors, community leaders, business owners, and individuals serving in the capacity of authority, which includes law enforcement officials. In order for us to respect others, we must first and foremost respect ourselves. When we demonstrate respect for others, our self-respect and self-confidence increases significantly. Our children are the future, and we must prepare them the best way we know how through education, work ethics, and self-discipline to ultimately serve in the capacity of those positions of authority to include community leaders, business owners, educators, law enforcement, lawyers, and judges. Our law enforcement agencies, prison facilities, political legislative organizations, and judicial systems will only change once we prepare our youth to serve as the future leaders of these positions with integrity, fortitude, ethics, and Christian virtues.

Politically speaking, our society attempts to cringe at the realities associated with America's involvement with pipelining our minorities to prison, which is attributed to the triad of our police officers, the judicial system, and the penitentiary system. The empty momentary concerns demonstrated is not only disturbing but damaging to the merits of this beautiful country. When we take into consideration that the United States of America was built from multidiverse races, religions, and origins of immigrants, slaves, and indentured servants, we would think that our respect for our predecessors would be elevated. We would think that in honor of all of the contributions from our ancestors and positive measures taken to advance equality and justice, these disparities and immoralities would dissipate over the years. Evidently, it is necessary for each and every one of us to implement measures that will increase justice and equality into every facet of our lives. Our citizenship carries a substantial amount of responsibility, and it also entitles us to the esteemed privilege of constitutional rights.

Our country is bonded by the threads of liberty, freedom, and equality, and our ethos of power are in relation to these collective stimuluses. Power can be viewed from various perspectives, but our initiatives should focus on instilling the presence of power in our youth. Our young adults will eventually lead our families, communities, and nation. The comprehension of an individual's capacity to influence others through purpose, direction, and motivation will equate their ability to sustain authority. Our society is protective of who we entrust with power, and those who strive for these critical positions throughout society have developed an elite attribute that enables them to respond accordingly.

Education is a critical cornerstone of power. If we can ignite the flames of interest in schooling, then we can catapult our youth's knowledge, skills, and abilities to lead with distinction. The ability to identify with leadership traits is attributed to a solid foundation of confidence and inspiration. We must mold our youth and young adults to challenge themselves to fulfill the roles associated with power throughout society. These positions of power are obtainable through vision, focus, and determination, and the only way we can expect change in our society is to change the incumbent mentality of society. We must place emphasis on the critical positions in society that impact our everyday struggles to include legislators, representatives, congresspersons, senators, lawyers, judges, police officers, scientists, physicians, economists, teachers, professors, firefighters, nurses, architects, media correspondents, etc. When we understand power, we respect it with the intent of displaying a sincere sense of appreciation for the capacity of the position.

Referent power is to embrace the role or position with the intent of personification and imitation.

Coercive power is to exercise the ability to implement consequences and or penalization for noncompliance.

Reward power is to exercise the ability to reward others for their actions, behaviors, or compliance.

Legitimate power is the acknowledgment of the capacity of a role or position of authority.

Expert power is the acknowledgment that power is the fruit of knowledge. "Knowledge is power."

Informational power is to exercise the power of being the sole proprietor of information.

Our leader's ability to utilize rational intellect throughout society is dependent upon their ability to embrace the social needs of our communities and understand the principal benefits versus the challenges associated with the economic, social, and industrial infrastructures within the local regions across our nation. We must continue to strategically arm our youth and young adults with knowledge and power to fulfill the roles of the leaders within society to exercise the appropriate powers to make a difference because "Anything we can Conceive, we can Achieve if we Believe."

Hilltop Thoughts:

- When we open our eyes, we realize there are many views from the same window.
- Thresholds are invitations to new beginnings.
- The exchange of kindness diminishes stereotypes.
- Just because a shoe fits does not mean we have to continue wearing it.
- Athletes stretch their muscles to increase performance and prevent injuries. We must stretch our faith to increase blessings and prevent complacency.
- Unfulfilled dreams are a result of unacceptable excuses.
- Challenges are designed to rearrange patterns of thought into resolutions of success.
- Cleared paths were once unknown quest. Mental explorations reveal adventurous destinations.
- Family trees are enriched by the soil of our values, blessed by roots of our ancestors, supported by the trunk of our history, nurtured by the branches of our lives bearing the fruits of our seeds.
- Our mental flashlights illuminate our dim crevices of unknown possibilities.
- Unfiltered thoughts have the propensity to taint the intent of the heart.
- The pursuit of our objectives resembles parallel parking, as we move forward, we identify open opportunities. We stop and begin planning the necessary adjustments. While maintaining situational awareness, we maneuver accordingly to achieve our objective(s).
- If we mentally visualize our positive, we will physically remove the negative.
- We control the gravitational force of success or failure; we are magnetized towards in life.
- Before you make plans, always get GOD's permission.

WHY BLACK LIVES MATTER

Beloved, let us love one another: for love is of GOD; and every one that loveth is born of GOD and knoweth GOD.

—1 John 4:7

I would like to welcome you to a chapter that may be difficult to read. Please take into consideration, it is even more challenging to live. Now let's take a mental voyage throughout history to allow me to describe the pain, suffering, and resilience of Black people. Our personal perceptions of what, why, and how we ever got to a point where it is necessary to inform the masses that "Black Lives Matter" is incomprehensible, evidently due to the inexplicable confusions of racial disparities has contributed to the innocent unconsciousness that has plagued our nation. The realness of reverse defines "if the shoe were on the other foot." This would illuminate the darkness of the subject with a new sense of comprehension, compassion, and comprehensive measures to implement awareness at every imaginable level.

Black Lives Matter because the psychological and physical abuse associated with a history of ancestral ties to slavery has contributed to the social paranoia of sharing the American entitlements of equality. Black's burdens of maltreatment, murders, and massacres began with the slave trade, "Anti-Literacy Laws" in 1740 to "Three-fifths Compromise 1787 to "Drapetomania" in 1851 to "Bleeding Kansas" in 1854 to the "Wilmington Massacre" in 1898 to the "Red Summer" in 1919 to "Black Wall Street" in Tulsa, Oklahoma, in

1921 to "Rosewood Massacre" in January 1923 to "Tuskegee Syphilis Experiment" in the 1932s to 1970s to the "FBI's COINTELPRO" in the 1956s to 1970s to the "16th Street Baptist Church Bombing" in 1963 to "Fire Hoses and Police Dogs" in 1963 to the "Assassination of Martin Luther King Jr." in 1968 to the "Beating of Rodney King Jr." in 1991 to the Murder of Trayvon Martin in 2012 to the "Execution of George Floyd" in 2020 to-to-to-too many atrocities to account for. The exploitation of Blacks throughout history has simmered to an inexcusable expectation amongst a people who have been forced into a familiarized state of inequality.

Black Lives Matter because the discriminative behaviors of unjust treatment based upon race is something that Blacks have been accustomed to since they emerged from the bowels of the slave ships and stepped onto American soil. When you have been exposed to distressing patterns of consistent mistreatment for such a long period of time, the pain begins to almost resemble the "Bear and the Bee Sting." The pain is present, but the bear endures the pain to acquire the honey. The atrocious acts of floggings, rape, amputations, lynching, branding, burns, mutilation, and confinement were unbearable, no pun intended. Through these difficult times, the Slave's "Honey" was their Freedom. Today Black's "Honey" is Justice and Equality.

Black Lives Matter because Black's resilience is unquestionable. They evolved from Slavery on Juneteenth, June 19, 1865, two years after President Lincoln's Emancipation Proclamation when Union General Gordan Granger led Federal troops through Galveston, Texas, and proudly announced the Union had conquered the confederacy and the slaves were free. Unfortunately, the discriminative mindset and behaviors instilled in the White race still existed, and they continued to torment Blacks as a signature of demanding respect. A free Black man was still considered less than equal to a White man. Failure to render the utmost respect, such as not addressing him as sir or looking him in his eyes, could result in unspeakable punishment.

Black Lives Matter because many freed slaves were financially incapable of providing for their families based upon the limited resources and equal opportunities in the south. A vast number of newly freed slaves were ultimately forced into positions of tenant farming or sharecropping, which benefited the landowner financially, since the loss of free slave labor, he could no longer maintain the large lots of land without assistance. In many instances, sharecroppers were taken advantage of through erroneous agreements, perpetual indebtedness, and manipulation to keep Blacks in an oppressed state to which benefited the White landowners. On the other hand, a large number of Black families decided to move to the North to pursue occupational opportunities to avoid the sharecropper's nightmares.

Black Lives Matter because the primary difference between the North and the South during these times was that the racism in the South was overt and attributed to white supremacy. In the South, racism was unapologetic and the Jim Crow laws reinforced the South's ideologies. In many ways, this was better than the North where covert racism existed through disguised measures of discriminatory acts that were actually evasive and subtle, enabling the objective to subliminally oppress Blacks in a manner that was deliberate in nature.

Black Lives Matter because when Blacks returned home from fighting in World War I, World War II, and the Vietnam War, they were instantaneously reacquainted with racism. Remnants of Jim Crow lingered throughout the American nation. Various degrees of racism inundated cities in the North and South. Blacks did not receive the GI Bill money promised to pursue educational or vocational goals, tuition assistance, or home mortgage benefits. Black families were strategically positioned in undesirable locations throughout the city, commonly referred to as ghettos, underprivileged, or urban neighborhoods through redlining and covenants. Health care and education were incomparable to the privileged White health care programs and educational institutes.

Black Lives Matter because all of these disproportionate factors have contributed over the years to the psychological challenges associated with an impoverished environment that creates social stigmas and prejudices across our nation. The psychological threat of another group of people attempting to slowly migrate to predominately White neighborhoods and impeding upon their resources, employment opportunities, schools, and way of life can be difficult to ingest. This may also have had a tremendous impact on White's cultural norms especially when racial agitation is embedded into the minds of the civil community through media, propaganda, and hate groups.

Black Lives Matter because false narratives, prejudices, hate, discrimination, oppression, and injustice have beleaguered our nation throughout history. We as Americans have the ability to stand firm on human principles and do the right thing, our values and beliefs will inspire us to strive to live in accordance with GOD's will.

> If a man says I love GOD and hateth his brother, he is a liar: for he that loveth not his brother whom he hath seen, how can he love GOD whom he hath not seen? (1 John 4:20)

The United States of America is exceptionally capable of being so much more than a question of *Do Black Lives Matter?* or *Do All Lives Matter?* As the parents of two amazing young men, Anthony II and Alyxandor, Aprile and I share equal love for both of them. If for some reason an unfortunate circumstance was to occur, causing physical, mental, or emotional anguish with one of our sons, regardless of which son, we will focus our attention in the direction of the son in immediate need of our attention. Our unconditional love for the other son has not decreased, diminished, or dispersed, it is temporarily focused on the son in need of immediate care. We have a parental responsibility to acknowledge the fact that there is a problem, and we have to address it immediately. There is absolutely no need to identify the significance of our other son. It is not worthy of conversation. We already know we love him, but the issue of concern needs to be addressed. Until it is resolved, his pain is our pain. If we do not confront his suffering, it could evolve into something more serious or possibly fatal.

What man of you, having a hundred sheep,
if he lose one of them, doth not leave the ninety
and nine in the wilderness and go after that which
is lost until he find it?" (Luke 15:4)

We, as a nation, have endured the suffering of allowing Blacks to be mistreated, murdered, and massacred without acknowledging the injustices and inequalities that have tormented this country throughout history. We as American citizens have a moral and ethical obligation to stand on the principles of the intent of the United States Constitution, the Declaration of Independence, and the Bill of Rights.

Black Lives Matter because Blacks have every right to fight for justice and equality in the same manner as the United States of America's Founding Fathers stood up to Britain when they had their knee on America's neck. Thomas Jefferson, one of the originals, was honored with the distinct privilege of writing the Declaration of Independence. The most fascinating historical document articulates the belief that "all men are created equal, and they are endowed by the Creator with certain unalienable rights to include life, liberty and the pursuit of happiness." But this beautiful illustration of the declaration carved into our American history was written by a prominent slave owner that did not bestow these Declaration of Independence privileges to his property, that being his slaves. These are the types of contradictions and historical devastations that haunt Blacks every day. Every person that believes that our country has come a long way is absolutely correct, unfortunately, from an origin of slavery to lynching to choke holds to unarmed shootings. We are a nation of opportunity, a federal republic, and a representative of democracy. We are a nation of immigrants illuminated by diversity, contributing to our global power. Black Lives Matter because united we stand, divided we fall, one nation under GOD, indivisible with liberty and justice for all. That is why we have to remember that "Anything you can Conceive, you can Achieve if you Believe."

Moment of silence…

EMMETT LOUIS TILL
GEORGE LEE
LAMAR SMITH
HERBERT LEE
WILLIE EDWARDS JR.
MACK CHARLES PARKER
CPL ROMAN DUCKSWORTH JR.
PAUL GUIHARD
MEDGAR EVERS
ADDIE MAE COLLINS
DENISE MCNAIR
CAROLE ROBERTSON
CYNTHIA WESLEY
VIRGIL LAMAR WARE
WILLIAM LOUIS MOORE
LOUIS ALLEN
HENRY HEZEKIAH DEE
CHARLES EDDI MOORE
JAMES EARL CHANEY
ANDREW GOODMAN
MICHAEL HENRY SCHWERNER
LT COL. LEMUEL PENN
BRUCE KLUNDER
MALCOM X
JIMMIE LEE JACKSON
JONATHAN MYRICK DANIELS
JAMES REEB
VIOLA GREGG LIUZZO
ONEAL MOORE
WILLIE BREWSTER
SAMUEL LEAMON YOUNGE JR.
VERNON F. DAHMER
BEN CHESTER WHITE
MARTIN LUTHER KING JR.

Wharlest Jackson
Benjamin Brown
Samuel E. Hammond Jr.
Delano Herman Middelton
Henry Ezekial Smith
James Earl Green
Phillip Lafayette Gibbs
Eric Garner
John Crawford III
Michaelbrown
Ezell Ford
Laquan Mcdonald
Dante Parker
Michelle Cusseaux
Tanisha Anderson
Akai Gurley
Victor Manuel Larosa
Oliver Jarrod Gregoire
Tamir Rice
George V. King
Dominique Franklin Jr.
Emerson Clayton Jr.
Rondre Lamar Hornbeak
Tommy Yancy
Quentin Bird
Yvette Smith
John Crawford III
Ricky Deangelo Hinkle
Wally Flex
Jerame C. Reid
Corey Levert Tanner
Tanisha Anderson
Zikarious Flint
Antoine Dominique Hunter
Jason Harrison
Charles Goodridge

GREGORY LEWIS TOWNS JR.
ANESSON JOSEPH
STEVEN ISBY
JUAN MAY
JUSTIN SULLIVAN
CHRISTOPHER MCCRAY
KENNETH CHRISTOPHER LUCAS
JACQUELINE NICHOLS
RONALD SINGLETON
ERNEST SATTERWHITE
HOWARD WALLACE BOWE JR.
FLORENCE WHITE
VERNICIA WOODARD
DEANGELO WOODS
TREON JOHNSON
KALDRICK DONALD
CAMERON TILLMAN
ROBERT BALTIMORE
JORDAN BAKER
HALLIS KINSEY
EDDIE RAY EPPERSON
EMANUEL JEAN-BAPTISE
DAVID ANDRE SCOTT
ASIA ROUNDTREE
EUGENE WILLIAMS
LAVON KING
CRAIG J. MCKINNIS
JOHN T. WILSON
WILLIE SAMS
ROBERT STORAY
ERIC RICKS
CEDRIC STANLEY
TYRONE DAVIS
JEREMY LAKE
LASHANO GILBERT
VICTOR WHITE II

David Yearby

Latandra Ellington

Christopher Jones

Arvel Douglas Williams

Rumain Brisbon

Mark Anthony Blocker

Balantine Mbegbu

Dustin Keith Glover

Matthew Walker

Tyree Woodson

Darrien Nathaniel Hunt

DeAndre Lioyd Starks

Jerome Dexter Christmas

Dennis Grisby

Michael Ricardo Minor

Iretha Lilly

Adam Madison

Dante Parker

Samuel Shields

D'Andre Berghardt Jr.

Briatay McDuffy

Anthony Bartley

Jeffrey Ragland

Jerry Brown

Keara Crowder

Donovan King

Brian Demarcus West

Justin Griffin

Leo Blackman Jr.

Briant Paula

Dontre Hamilton

Frank Smart

Natasha McKenna

Tony Robinson

Mya Hall

Anthony Hill

PHILLIP WHITE
ERIC HARRIS
WILLIAMAM CHAPMAN II
WALTER SCOTT
BRENDON GLENN
CHRISTIAN TAYLOR
JONATHAN SANDERS
SALVADO ELLSWOOD
SAMUEL DUBOSE
SANDRA BLAND
KEITH HARRISON MCLEOD
ALBERT JOSEPH DAVIS
PATERSON BROWN
DARRIUS STEWART
MICHAEL SABBIE
ASSHAMS PHAROAH MANLEY
FELIX KUMI
JUNIOR PROSPER
LAMONTEZ JONES
KIETH CHILDRESS
BETTIE JONESBETT
KEVIN MATTHEWS
MICHAEL NOEL
LEROY BROWNING
ROY NELSON
MIGUEL ESPINAL
NATHANIEL PICKETT
TIARA THOMPSON
CORNIELUS BROWN
JAMAR CLARK
RICHARD PERKINS
MICHAEL LEE MARSHALL
ALONZO SMITH
ANTHONY ASHFORD
DOMINIC HUTCHINSON
RAYSHAUN COLE

CHRISTOPHER KIMBLE
KEITH MCLEOD
WAYNE WHEELER
LA'VANTE BIGGS
JAMES CARNEY III
TYREE CRAWFORD
INDIA KAGER
ASSHAMS MANLEY
BRIAN KEITH DAY
BILL Y RAY DAVIS
GEORGE MANN
SAMUEL DUBOSE
JONATHAN SANDERS
FREDDIE BLUE
VICTO LAROSA III
SPENCER MCCAIN
ZAMIEL CRAWFORD
KEVIN BAJOIE
JERMAINE BENJAMIN
KRIS JACKSON
KEVIN HIGGENBOTHAM
ROSS ANTHONY
CURTIS JORDAN
RICHARD GREGORY
MARKUS CLARK
LORENZO HAYES
DE'ANGELO STALLWORTH
DAJUAN GRAHAM
BRANDON GLENN
REGINALD MOORE
NUWNAH LAROCHE
JASON CHAMPION
BRIAN OVERSTREET
DAVID FELIX
SAMUEL HARRELL
TERRY LEE CHATMAN

Freddie Gray
Norman Cooper
Brian Acton
Darrell Brown
Frank Shephard III
Walter Scott
Donald Dontay IV
Jason Moland
Dominick Wise
Philip White
Bobby Gross
Denzel Brown
Brandon Jones
Askari Roberts
terrance Moxley
Anthony Hill
Bernard Moore
Naeschylus Vinzant
Charly Africa Keunang
Darrell Gatewood
Deontre dorsey
Thomas Allen Jr.
Gerdie Moise
Lavall Hall
Calvon Reid
Terry Price
Natasha McKenna
Jeremy Lett
Artago Damon Howard
Kevin Garrett
Alvin Haynes
Tiano Meton
Leslie Sapp
Andre Lamone Murphy Sr.
Germonta Wallace
Matthew Ajibade

Eric Senegal
Alexia Christian
Joseph Mann
Troy Robinson
Gerals Hall
Jamal Rollins
James Rich
Terrance Thomas
Anthony Eddington
Ryan Joseph
Marlon Lewis
Lavar Douglas
Earl Eubanks
Waltki Williams
Redrick Batiste
Mark Hicks
David Crosby-Dowdy
Norman Gary
Bruce Johnson II
Jason Stringer
Irecas Valentine
Abdul Artan
Jerome Harmon
Terrel Walker
Richard Grimes
Cloetha Mitchell
Kajuan Raye
Talif Scudder
George Bush III
Ivory Pantallion
Frank Clark
Eric Brito
Darious Jones
Samspson Fleurant
Joshua Beal
Dontrell Carter

RASHEEN SINGLETARY
ANDRW DEPEIZA
MICHELLE SHIRLEY
RITCHIE HARBISON
DARRYL CHISOLM
FERGUSON LAURENT
KEENAN BRADLEY
TERRENCE COLEMAN
JASON KING
THAD HALE
DARIUS WIMBERLY
MALCOM HICKSON
ROY RICHARDS
AARON BALLARD
LARRY MATTHEWS
DEMARIUS MOORE
DEBORAH DANNER
KIRK FIGUEROA
DERIC BROWN
JAQUAR MATHIS
CHRISTOPHER SHAKLEFORD
DONTE JONES
ODDIS COLVIN JR.
CARNELL SNELL JR.
REGINALD THOMAS
NAJIER SALAAM
KADEEM TROTTER
JACQUARIOUS ROBINSON
GEORGE RICHARDS-MEYERS
DOUGLAS RAINEY
NICHOLAS GLENN
CHRISTOPHER SOWELL
ALFRED OLANGO
KEITH SCOTT
PHILIP HASAN
DAHIR ADAN

Terrence Crutcher
Tyre King
Markell Bivens
Terence Sterling
Robert Brown
Gregory Frazier
Sadiq Idris
Moses Ruben
Jerome Damon
Michael Thompson Jr.
Alfred Toe
Levonia Riggins
Jaquan Terry
Donia Taylor
Kelley Forte
Brandon Koles
Colby Friday
Omer Ismail
Kenny Watkins
Kendrick Brown
Fred Barlow
Darnell Wicker
Jamarion Robinson
Jawari Porter
Earl Shaleek Pickney
Demarco Newman
Korryn Gaines
Joyce Quaweay
Donnell Thomson Jr.
Paul O'neal
Jeffery Smithy
Devon Martes
Dalvin Holloway
Richard Risher
Gavin Long
Jeffery Tyson

Bernard Wells III
Austin Howard
Orville Edwards
Derek Love
Jermaine Johnson
Dayten Harper
Deangelo Webb
Jason Brooks
Tyler Gebhard
Andre Johnson
Carlos Brown
Alva Braziel
Ernest Fells
Sidney Washington
Lafayette Evans
Delrawn Small
Jai Williams
Kawme Patrick
Tyrone Reado
Sherman Evans
Germichael Kennedy
Donte Johnson
Deravis Caine Rogers
Ismael Miranda
Jay Anderson
Angelo Brown
Gary Porter
Clarence Howard
John Williams
Antwun Shumpert
Michael Moore
Lyndarius Witherspoon
Kieth Bursey
John Brisco
Demarco Rhymes
Willis Walker

Henry Green
William Meat-Meat James
Rodney Smith
Michael Johnson
Dennis Hudson
Osee Calix
Ollie Brooks
Devonte Gates
Terry Frost
Doll Pierre-Lewis
Joshua Beebee
Vernell Bing Jr.
Michael Wilson
Kentrill Carraway
Jessica Williams
Jabril Robinson
Jaffort Smith
Sean Mondragon
Arthur DaRosa
Arthur Williams Jr.
Lionel Gibson
Alton Witchard
Burt Johnson
Ronald Willimas
Deresha Armstrong
MAtthew Tucker
Reginald Dogan
Charlin Charles
Joshua Brooks
Ashtian Barnes
Richard Bard Jr.
Terril Thomas
Demarcus Semur
Willie Tillman
Jorevis Scruggs
Rico Johnson

DEMETRIUS DORSEY
KISHA ARRONE
GEORGE TILLMAN
EDSON THEVENIN
CAMERON GLOVER
ROBERT HOWARD
RODNEY WATTS
PIERRE LOURY
JAMES SIMPSON
MARY TRUXILLO
QURON WILLIAMS
DIAHLO GRANT
JERMON SEALS
LAMONT GULLEY
DAZION JEROME FLENAUGH
LARONDA SWEAT
ROBERT DENTMOND
KEVIN HICKS
DARIUS ROBINSON
MATTHEW WOOD JR.
KIMANI JOHNSON
JAMES BROWN III
DERIANTE MILLER
DOMINIQUE SILVA
ALEXO ALLEN
TORREY ROBINSON
THURMAN REYNOLDS
INDIA BEATY
TRAVIS STEVESON
SCOTT BENNETT
CHRISTOPHER NELMS
LAMAR HARRIS
CHE TAYLOR
JACAI COLSON
PETER GAINES
MARCO LOUD

Calvin Smith
Keith Montgomery Jr.
Tyre Privott
Arteair Porter Jr.
Sahlah Ridgeway
Akiel Denkins
Kionte Spencer
Greg Gunn
Jerand Ross
Cedric Ford
Christopher Davis
Marquintan Sandlin
Kisha Michael
Paul Gaston
Dyzawn Perkins
Calin Roquemore
Ali Yahia
Peter Fanfan
Mohamed Barry
Shalamar Lewis
Eric Harris
David Joseph
Randy Nelson
Marese Collins
Wendell Celestine
Peter John
Charles Smith
Bruce Kelley
Rodney Turner
Randolph McClain
Christopher Drew
Christopher Kelonji
Bennilee Tignor
Jonathan Bratcher
Janet Wilson
Cedric Norris

Jordan Edwards
Timothy Albert
Crayton West
Henry Bennett
Stephon Clark
Rakeem Bentley
Carlton Murphy
Tymar Crawford
Michael Lee Marshall
Quintonio Legrier
Antronie Scott
Aaron Bailey
Ronell Foster
Antwon Roseii
Botham Jean
Pamela Turner
Sincere Pierce
Dominique Clayton
Atatiana Jefferson
Christopher Whitfield
Ronald Greene
Charleena Chavon Lyles
Charleena's Unborn Child
Alfred Olango
Michael Lorenzo Dean
Christopher Mccorvey
Bijan Ghaisar
Casey Goodson
Dijon Kizzee
Charles Roundtree Jr.
Tony McDade
Emantic Fitgerald Bradford Jr.
William Howard Green
Javier Ambler
Sterling Higgins
Gregory Edwards

Marcellis Stinette
Angelo "AJ" Crooms
Manuel Ellis
Marcellis Stinnette
William Green
John Elliot Neville
Elijah McClain
Angelo Quinto
Maurice Hill
Jonathan D. Price
Rayshard Brooks
Patrick Warren Sr.
Vincent Belmonte
Carlos Carson
Marvin David Scott
Aura Rosser
David McAtee
Dreasjon Reed
Michael Brent Ramos
George Floyd
Butch Armstead
Breonna Taylor
Damian Daniels
Trayford Pellerin
Jacob Blake
Daniel Prude
Casey Goodson Jr.
Deon Kaye
Sincere Pierce
Rodney Applewhite
Joshua Feast
Aj Crooms
Donovan Lynch
Andre Hill
Ma Khia Bryant
Andrew Brown Jr.

Daunte Wright
Ronald Greene

Unfortunately, this list has extended since the publishing of this book, and it will continue to increase until we as a nation recognize why BLACK LIVES MATTER.

Why Hilltop Lives Matter...

LaRue Crain Sr.
Frances Crain
Gertha Thorn
Alice Thorn
LaRue Crain Jr.
Delores Crain
Acey Lovett Jr.
Gertha Lovett
Sandee Stewart
Troy Robinson
Mary Easter-Daniels
Leonard "Sonny" Kelly
Dowell Thorn
Dowell Davis Thorn III
Lionel Swift Sr.
Elenora Swift
Jawuan Swift
Larhonda Hardy
James E. Cain Sr.
Janelle Cain
Curtis L. Dudley Sr.
Virginia Dudley
Kasandra Moffett
Daniel Vaughan
Benjamin Iaasic
David Crittendon
Bernard Houston

Jerry Lee Jackson
Donald Langford Sr.
Juanita Langford
Tina Langford
Donna Langford
Leroy Turner
Derek Bayless
John Carpenter IV
Jimmy Kelly
Jimmy Smith
Marlene Milligan
Tyrone Doss
Tacoma Parker
Ronnie Joe Ryan
Marco Rios
Eugene Carr
Dwayne Hill
Damon Williams
Derrick Williams
Michael Clark
Jonathan Robinson
Robert Doss II
Kunta Kinte Jones
Denise McField
Catherine McField
Tommy Brock Jr.
Judy Brock
Marvin Scott
Eugene Mobley
Roger O Laskey
Sam Daniels
Chyna Thomas
Lee Bertha Thomas
Ora Jean Andrews
Ann Lee
Earl Goodlow

Hortencia Refour
Dave Brown
Leo Brown
Edna Travis
Raymond Cain
Thomas Westbrook
Ivory Crittendon Sr.
Carylon Ryan
Vernessa Ryan
Johnny Bumphus
Keria Henderson
Shirley Law
Rochelle Baker
James Cobb
Jim Cobb
Mary Cobb
Margo Cunningham
Akee Redic
Geno Franks
Wanda Lewis
James Waller
Andre Bennett
Pearl Thierry
Dwayne Patterson
Derrick Lee
Deloris Coty
Bernice Watkins
Nicole Jackson
Rocky Dallas
Ruby Gray
Quincy Walker
Virginia Taylor
Harold Moss
John Webb
James Brown
Angela Jackson

Edward Brown
Shelly Waller
Shelly Williams
Kimberly McDuffie
Irvin Hooper
Andre Fountain
David Johnson
Darnell Parks
Alberta Canada
David Montgomery
Phillip Montgomery
Louise Jordan
Willie James Moffett
Jefferey Singletary
Seneca Hopkins
Hessie Baines Sr.
Hessie Baines Jr.
Paul Chase
Ernest Rynes
Clifford Krenkowski
Curtis Jones Jr.
Anthony Davis Jr.
Charlesetta Weston
Jack Tanner
Rocky Lockridge
Michael Ward
Mondel McCain
Frankie Houston
Robert McCain
Parish Johnson
David McKinney
Kimbery Joyce
Everett Watkins
Morris McCollum
Alonzo Foote
James Givens

Kenneth Boyd
Rory Williams
Jasper Ervin
Andre Lamar
Nikiner Tublin
Quincy Walker
Chuckie Webb
Peter James
Tyrone Cross
Kenneth Boyd
Jeremy Rollins
Martino Smith
Deymon Price
Quincy Oneal
Jerome Satterwhite
Quantika Grisby
James McCullough
Carlos Beal
Levi Mack
Tacoma Hayes
Howard Hare
Gary Brown
Tony Salter
Fred Bailey
Meeka Willingham
Jamie Howard
Hank Rivers
Dante Robinson
Devondre Davis
Jahleen Mitchell
Lee Waller-Cubean
Otis Banks
Billy Seats
Amaryllis Denise Swanigan
Mark Bass
Vermond Lovelace

Ozell Tyrece Tate
Deangelo Reese
Bruce Randall Johnson II
Phillip Ryan Jr.
Hyson Sabb
Charles Williams
Emmit Taylor Jr.
Stanley Howard
Barbara Driscoll
Reggie Bryant
Melanie Horton
Tyliah Young
Earnesteen Randolph
Albert Merriweather
Peter J. Quins
Pearl Thierry
Tino Smith
Nelson Williams
Harriet Williams
Coma Cummins
Shirley Hooper
Melva Taylor-Williams
Rodrick Smith
Acey Andre Stewart

Please accept my apology if your loved one is not listed above. Everyone listed and those not listed were part of the Hilltop fabric that held our community together. May they rest in peace knowing that we will continue to uplift, support, and respect the Hilltop of Tacoma, Washington, because "Anything you can Conceive, you can Achieve if you Believe."

Justice for Jawuan Swift...

SERENITY

God grant me the serenity
To accept the things I cannot change;
Courage to change the things I can;
And wisdom to know the difference.
Living one day at a time;
Enjoying one moment at a time;
Accepting hardships as the pathway to peace;
Taking, as He did, this sinful world
As it is, not as I would have it;
Trusting that He will make all things right
If I surrender to His Will;
So that I may be reasonably happy in this life
And supremely happy with Him
Forever and ever in the next.
Amen.

—Karl Paul Reinhold Niebuhr

My relationship with God has increased my faith, strengthened my hope, enhanced my life, and without question, it has also given me a new perspective on the importance of my serenity. Throughout life, we eventually grow to comprehend the consequences of our actions, causing us to realize that we must implement the appropriate changes in our thoughts, actions, and behaviors in efforts of moving in the direction of new beginnings. Every year, we establish new resolutions with the intent of a fresh start in order to conquer unhealthy or unproductive habits and achieve future goals. Allow me to introduce you to a new and improved reality. We don't have to wait 365 days to motivate ourselves to increase. Every day that we place our feet on the ground, open our eyes, or take the next breath is an opportunity to receive and acknowledge our blessings from above. Every day is an opportunity to accept new challenges with faith. My faith allows me to lean on the Lord whenever I'm in need of assistance for myself, family, friends, or acquaintances.

My faith encourages me to accept the things I cannot change by the realization that things could always be worse. Today someone will lose their mother, father, grandmother, grandfather, uncle, aunt, niece, nephew, son, daughter, grandson, granddaughter, husband, wife, or someone they knew in life. Today someone will lose their life to cancer, diabetes, heart failure, stroke, cirrhosis, tuberculosis, or the coronavirus. Today someone will lose their life in a fire, car accident, violent attack. Today a young man will be violated by another man in prison. Today a young girl will be sexually assaulted by a family member. If none of these things happened to us today, this should remind us that we are blessed. Regardless of the current circumstances, things can always be worse. Our genuine attitude of gratitude and positive outlook on life supports our appreciation for the joy of peacefulness and tranquility. Our positive state of mind breathes calmness into our responses when difficulties arise.

Life is happening all around us, and we have the ability to magnetize the pleasures of family, relationships, journeys, and accomplishments. This is achieved by adopting a mindset of thankfulness for what life has to offer. If we sat down for five minutes and performed a positive assessment of our family and friends, how many of them would make the cut? Ask yourself: By going down the list of your family members and close friends, who inspires, coaches, encourages, uplifts, and prays for me? These are the questions that will enable us to eliminate the negativity from our lives. The sooner we are able to grasp the fact that certain people do not have our best interest at heart, the sooner we can focus our attention on the positive relationships in our life. It may not be possible to physically remove people from our lives, but we have the power to control the distance of the relationships.

Someone once told me that if you see a crowd of nine losers congregating and you join the group, eventually there will be ten. My positive mental state allows me to flip the equation to winners as opposed to losers. This inspires me to surround myself with positivity. We must identify the winners from the beginners and distant ourselves from the losers. I choose the benefits of optimism over the iniquities of pessimism. As I awake to another day to appreciate my blessings, I begin the day with reading a scripture. Next I listen to some spiritual motivation with Pastor T. D. Jakes from The Potter's House, Reverend Dr. Anthony R. Young from the New Creation AME Church, or Pastor Bryan Briggs from Destination Church. Seeing how I like to mix it up some days, I also listen to various motivational speakers such as Les Brown, Eric Thomas, Billy Alsbrooks, Earl Nightingale, David Goggins, Daymond John, Denzel Washington, Zig Zigglar, and there are several others. My point is that I consciously start my day off on a positive note. The beginning of my day is the foundation of my attitude. My mental state choreographs the serenity I strive to embrace daily. I have an individual responsibility to define peace within me. Through faith, hope, and prayers, I've been able to fortify my relationship with my Lord and Savior. Our spiritual bond strengthens our confidence and naturally contributes to our overall serenity. I have been able to establish a spiritual force field around me by utilizing my virtues of conviction. Growing up, I unfortunately gravitated toward misfortunes and regrettable behaviors. As I have matured over the years, I have grown to appreciate the benefits of serenity.

My newfound attraction to goodwill, integrity, and gratitude has inspired my explorations of a constructive consciousness. My willingness to feed the positive and starve the negative has allowed me to increase immeasurably. My blessings have flourished in multitudes in comparison to living a life of gloom, blame, distrust, and pessimism. If we fertilize our faith with the nutrients of confidence, contributions, and courage, this will boost the swags that substantiates. What we sow is what we shall also reap.

My confidence in myself, my abilities, and my judgment sustain my serenity. The appreciation for the importance of contributing to others includes personal time, professional assistance, spiritual guidance, and financial advisory support. These are just a couple of the essential nutrients that result in self-fulfilling rewards. Let us not forget, the importance of my courage to accept the things I cannot change allows me to process misfortunes with cultivated comprehension. The absence of negative energy is purposefully replaced and substituted with a mindset of turning negatives into positives. My courage extinguishes fear, distress, and anxiety with a genuine trust in GOD that "this too shall pass." I was once told that "worrying is like a rocking chair. It gives you something to do, but it doesn't get you anywhere" (Van Wilder). Many of us waste precious time of our lives focusing on troubles, challenges, and societal concerns, whereas that time could be redirected to productive scenarios and creative solutions. My understanding of the magnitude of confidence, contributions, and courage is a gift that I treasure and depend upon daily to disintegrate the things that attempt to invade my feng shui.

Serenity and courage contribute to my optimistic attitude. My wisdom to know the difference inspires me to make a difference. I personally admire how Judge Gregory Mathis is able to mentor, lecture, chastise, and educate the community from his platform of televised justice. I respect his ability to associate himself with the challenges of societal and economic disparities growing up, but he did not allow the circumstances to dictate his purpose in life. I have come to the realization that my life is not dictated by my disparities, but it is directed by my choices, decisions, and behaviors. My insight, perceptions, and experiences motivate me to utilize my GOD-given talents in addition to common sense to avoid the perils of distraction, disruption, and destruction. The ability to steer clear of negativity allows my mental GPS to guide me to a peaceful mindset. Regardless of the challenges I faced on the Hilltop and throughout life, I have been blessed with the drive, knowledge, and capabilities to identify and embrace the benefits of positive outlooks and a serene lifestyle.

The center of my happiness is surrounded by the joy of my faith and my ability to look on the other side of misfortune and trust in the Lord. The signature of my strength is substantiated by my catalogue of virtues I strive to uphold during good times and bad. My overall description of heightened strategies to excel one day at a time is based upon the principles of living my best life as opposed to focusing on yestermoments and/or the untelling future. Today I am in control of my physical and mental position in life My cerebral capacity allows me to navigate the journeys of life's grid in accordance with peaceful parameters.

> Yea, though I walk through the valley of the
> shadow of death, I will fear no evil. (Psalms 23:4)

GOD's word is applicable in every aspect of our being. My spiritual relationship with GOD encourages me that I can walk through life's valleys because I am protected from the calamities of evil. I should and shall live in the moment and enjoy the blessings bestowed upon me. I will embrace all that is good and preserve my joy by continuing to perform random acts of kindness, serve as my brother's keeper, and surrender my ways of thinking, acting, and feeling in accordance with the will of GOD. The very moment that I was able to place a value on my serenity was when I first learned to treasure what is truly important in life. The Lord has enriched me with the knowledge of realizing that you should never love anything that cannot love you back.

I treasure my roots. I treasure my trials and triumphs. I treasure my Hilltop family and friends. I treasure my relationship with GOD who provides me the precious gift of serenity. My goal is to inspire others to assume control of their thoughts, actions, and behaviors. I will encourage others to realize that our story of tribulations is His glory. My pitfalls have allowed me to accept responsibility for my actions and learn from my mistakes. Each of these tests have ascended into trustworthy testimonies that allow unbelievers to realize the blessings of the Lord. I pray that each of us are willing to humbly ask for forgiveness from the Lord and pray for salvation.

My Father, I come before you as a sinner. I believe in my heart Jesus Christ died for my sins. I believe in the resurrection that Jesus rose from the dead. I pray that you save me and give me everlasting life.

This prayer saved my life, and it will save yours too. I am praying for your continued blessings and sovereign serenity. Glory be to GOD and may you always remember, "Anything you can Conceive, you can Achieve if you Believe."

ABOUT THE AUTHOR

Anthony L. Crain is a native of Hilltop Tacoma, Washington. He earned his diploma from Henry Foss High School. He received his associate degree from Central Texas College, earning his certification as a basic mental health professional. He received his bachelor degree in human resources management from Trident University. He married the former Aprile Jordan in 1987. They have two sons, Anthony II, and Alyxandor (wife: Laura). He retired with honors from the United States Army with 22 years of distinguished service. Anthony is a member of the fraternal organizations, Prince Hall Free and Accepted Masons and the Ancient Egyptian Arabic Order Nobles Mystic Shrine. Anthony currently serves as a government contractor, as a logistics specialist, and New Equipment Trainer in support of Program Manager Soldier Survivability. He also serves as an alcohol and substance abuse and anger management group facilitator for the Center for Therapeutic Justice and the Riverside Criminal Justice Agency. Anthony's philosophy on life is, "Anything you can Conceive, you can Achieve, if you Believe."